THE GREAT
AZUSA
STREET REVIVAL

THE GREAT
AZUSA
STREET REVIVAL

THE LIFE AND SERMONS OF
WILLIAM SEYMOUR

COMPILED BY ROBERTS LIARDON

WHITAKER
HOUSE

Unless otherwise indicated, all Scripture quotations are taken from the King
James Version of the Holy Bible. Scripture quotations marked (RV) are taken from
the Revised Version of the Holy Bible.

THE GREAT AZUSA STREET REVIVAL
The Life and Sermons of William Seymour

Roberts Liardon Ministries
P.O. Box 781888
Orlando, FL 32878
www.RobertsLiardon.com

ISBN: 978-1-64123-522-8
eBook ISBN: 978-1-64123-523-5

Printed in the United States of America
© 2020 by Roberts Liardon

Whitaker House
1030 Hunt Valley Circle
New Kensington, PA 15068
www.whitakerhouse.com

Library of Congress Control Number: 2020947547

3 4 5 6 7 8 9 10 11 12 **W** 27 26 25 24 23

CONTENTS

William J. Seymour, pastor of the Azusa Street Mission

PART ONE

CATALYST OF CHANGE

A BIOGRAPHY OF
WILLIAM J. SEYMOUR

Roberts Liardon

Serving as the "catalyst" of the Pentecostal movement in the twentieth century, William J. Seymour turned a tiny Los Angeles horse stable on Azusa Street into an international center of revival. Because the baptism of the Holy Spirit, with the evidence of speaking in tongues, was a major part of the meetings held there, Seymour became the leader of the first organized movement that promoted this experience. At Azusa, blacks, whites, Hispanics, and Europeans all met and worshiped together, crossing formerly impossible cultural lines. Although the success of the revival was short-lived, we still enjoy its fruits. Today, Azusa remains a common word within God's household.

The Azusa Street Mission produced some wild stories. Time was of little concern to these Pentecostal pioneers who would often pray all night for another's deliverance. They believed the Word of God and waited for its manifestation.

In every situation that arose, the seekers made a demand on the Word's authority. If insects tried to destroy someone's crops, believers at Azusa marched out to the field and declared the Word of God over their crops and the insects! In every recorded account, the insects stayed where they were told and didn't cross field borders. If they were destroying a neighbor's crops, they remained about twenty yards away from the believer's crops.

In another story, a large group of firemen came rushing into the Azusa Street Mission during a service, carrying fire hoses to extinguish a fire. But they never found one! Neighbors of the mission had seen a light that led them to believe the building was engulfed in flames, so they called the fire department. However, what they had actually seen was the glory of God.[1]

EYE OF THE TIGER

Centerville, Louisiana, is a southern bayou town only a few miles from the Gulf of Mexico. On May 2, 1870, a son was born in Centerville to Simon and Phyllis Seymour. They had been freed from slavery just a few years earlier, so William Joseph was born into a world of horrible racial violence. The Ku Klux Klan had been on the rampage for years. The Jim Crow laws had been established to prohibit all blacks from any social justices. And segregation was prevalent, even in the church.

Once freed from slavery, William Seymour's parents continued working on the plantation. As Seymour grew, he followed in their footsteps. Undaunted by the lack of formal education, like many others, he taught himself primarily through reading the Bible.

Seymour found his identity in Jesus Christ, believing that the Lord was the only liberator of mankind. He was a sensitive, high-spirited youth, and hungry for the truth of God's Word. It is said he experienced divine visions, and that early in life, he began to look for the return of Jesus Christ.[2]

At the age of twenty-five, Seymour finally broke through the mental bondage of his inferiority complex. Then doing what few black men dared, he left the homelands of southern Louisiana and headed north to Indianapolis, Indiana.

According to the U.S. Census of 1900, only 10 percent of the black race had ever left the South. But Seymour was determined that man-made shackles would never hold him.

SAINTS AND SMALLPOX

Unlike the rural South, Indianapolis was a thriving city that offered a number of opportunities. But many businesses still closed their doors to the black population, so Seymour could only find work as a hotel waiter.

Not long after his arrival, Seymour joined the Simpson Chapel Methodist Episcopal Church. This branch of Northern Methodists had a strong evangelistic outreach to all classes that appealed to Seymour. The church's example helped Seymour to further formulate his beliefs. To him, it was becoming ever more evident that there was no class or color line in the redemption of Jesus Christ.

However, it wasn't long before the racial lines hardened in Indianapolis. So Seymour moved to Cincinnati, Ohio. There, he continued to attend a Methodist church, but soon noticed that their doctrine was hardening as well. He was an avid follower of John Wesley, who believed in strong prayer, holiness, divine healing, and that there should be no discrimination in Jesus Christ. But it seemed the Methodists were moving away from their original roots.

In his search for a church, Seymour stumbled upon the Evening Light Saints, which would later become known as the Church of God Reformation Movement. The group didn't use musical instruments. They didn't wear rings or makeup. And they didn't dance or play cards. Even though it seemed like a religion of *no's*, the group was extremely happy. They found joy in their faith in difficult times as well as good.[3]

Seymour was warmly received by the Saints. It was in this setting that he received the call to ministry. Seymour wrestled with his calling and was fearful to answer. In the midst of his struggle, he contracted smallpox, which was usually fatal in that era. He survived three weeks of horrible suffering and was left with blindness in his left eye and severe facial scarring.

Seymour felt his contraction of the disease was a result of refusing the call of God. So he immediately submitted to the plan of God and was ordained through the Evening Light Saints. Soon he began traveling as an itinerant evangelist and provided his own financial support. In those days, few ministers asked for offerings. And Seymour, like many in his circle, believed that God was his provider. He believed that if God called him, then God would support him.

SPEAKING IN TONGUES...TODAY?

Seymour left Cincinnati and traveled to Texas, evangelizing along the way. When he arrived in Houston, he found family there, so he decided to make Houston his ministry base. In the summer of 1905, evangelist Charles F. Parham was holding crusades in Bryn Hall, which was located in downtown Houston. Each evening after the traffic had cleared, Parham and his helpers would march downtown in spectacular Holy Land clothing, carrying their "Apostolic Faith Movement" banner. Newspapers wrote positively about Parham's meetings, often giving them headlines.[4]

Houston was a city of cultural variety, so all races were drawn to Parham's meetings. A woman friend of Seymour's, Mrs. Lucy Farrow, attended Parham's meetings regularly, and had developed a pleasant relationship with the revivalist's family. Parham offered her the position of governess with his family if she would accompany them to Kansas, where they lived. Farrow was the pastor of a small Holiness church, but her love for Parham's family and her spiritual hunger motivated her to go. Upon her acceptance, she asked Seymour if he would pastor the church in

Charles F. Parham

her absence. He agreed to do so until she returned two months later with the Parham family.

When Mrs. Farrow returned to Houston, she told Seymour about her wonderful spiritual encounters in the Parham home—including her experience of speaking in tongues. Seymour was very moved by her experience, but he questioned the doctrine. He would eventually accept it, though he himself wouldn't speak in tongues for some time.[5] The Evening Light Saints didn't approve of Seymour's new theology, so he left the group, still never having spoken in tongues. Then Charles Parham announced the opening of his Bible school in Houston that December and Mrs. Farrow vehemently insisted that Seymour attend. Moved by her fervency and his own growing interest, Seymour enrolled.

Parham's school in Houston was set up much like the one in Topeka, Kansas. It was a communal-type living arrangement in one house, where the students and their instructor spent days and nights together, praying and studying the Word in an informal fashion. The students were not required to pay tuition, but did have to believe God for their own needs. Due to the culturally accepted practice of the day, it is questionable whether Seymour was allowed to stay overnight. Parham was moved by Seymour's hunger for the Word. And it is my belief, though very welcomed by Parham, that Seymour was only a daytime student. Though Seymour did not embrace every doctrine that Parham taught, he did embrace the truth of Parham's doctrine concerning Pentecost. He soon developed his own theology from it.

IN THE BEGINNING

After completing his studies at Parham's school, the events that led Seymour to Los Angeles started to quickly take place. In early 1906, Seymour began making plans to start a new Pentecostal church in which he could preach his newfound doctrine. Then he unexpectedly received a letter from Miss Neely Terry. Terry, who had been visiting relatives in Houston, had attended the church where Seymour pastored in place of Lucy Farrow. When she returned to California, she didn't forget Seymour's gentle and secure leadership. In her letter, Miss Terry asked Seymour to come to Los Angeles and pastor a congregation that had broken away from a Nazarene church. Believing the letter revealed his destiny, Seymour packed his bags and left for California in late January. Later he would write:

> It was the divine call that brought me from Houston, Texas, to Los Angeles. The Lord put it on the heart of one of the saints in Los Angeles to write me that she felt the Lord would have me come there, and I felt it was the leading of the Lord. The Lord provided the means and I came to take charge of a mission on Santa Fe Street.[6]

THE SPIRITUAL CONDITION OF THE CITY

A spiritual hunger was stirring in Los Angeles. There was a deep desire and longing for something to happen.

There was evidence of a spiritual revival even before Seymour arrived. Turn-of-the-century evangelists had spread the fire of God throughout Southern California and many groups of people were praying and witnessing throughout the city door to door. In fact, the entire city was on the verge of a great spiritual happening as many Los Angeles congregations of Christians were earnestly seeking God.

In 1906, Los Angeles was a microcosm of the world. Racial discrimination was rarely practiced because every culture, from Chinese to Hispanic, flocked to the city.

One particular group, the First Baptist Church of Los Angeles, was waiting for the return of their pastor, Rev. Joseph Smale. He had been on a three-week trip to Wales to sit under the great Welsh evangelist, Evan Roberts. Smale was on fire for God and was hoping to bring the same revival that had visited Wales home with him to Los Angeles.

Another evangelist and journalist, Frank Bartleman, shared a similar vision and joined with his church in prayer. Bartleman wrote to Roberts for revival instructions. One response from the Welshman ended this way: "I pray God to hear your prayer, to keep your faith strong, and to save California."

From these letters, Bartleman said he received the gift of faith for the revival to come. And he went on to believe that the prayers from Wales had much to do with God's outpouring in California, later saying, "The present worldwide revival was rocked in the cradle of little Wales."[7]

In Los Angeles, a small black group hungry for more of God had formed to worship. The leader of this new group was

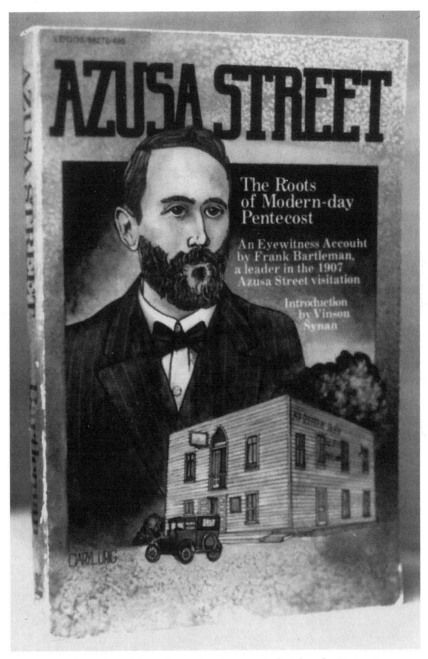

Frank Bartleman's book *Azusa Street: The Roots of Modern-day Pentecost.*

Sister Julia Hutchinson. She taught sanctification in a way that wasn't in agreement with her church's doctrine. Consequently, the pastor expelled the families involved with her teaching, who would eventually form a group with Seymour as pastor.

The group wasn't discouraged. They quickly banded together in the home of Mr. and Mrs. Richard Asbery, then grew so large that they were forced to rent a small mission hall on Santa Fe Street. Along with this growth came the desire for a change in leadership. The group felt a stranger to the Los Angeles area could be more effective, believing that he would command more respect among them. And Neely Terry, the Asberys' cousin, believed there could be only one man for the job. After praying about it, they all agreed to extend the invitation to Seymour.

BREAKING THE MESSAGE IN

Seymour arrived in Los Angeles, where there was already a citywide revival climate. It seemed to validate his sense of destiny. The large group assembled, eager to hear Seymour's first sermon; he expounded powerfully on the gospel of divine healing and the soon return of Christ. He then began his message from Acts 2:4 on speaking in other tongues. He taught that a person is not baptized in the Holy Spirit unless he or she speaks with other tongues. And he admitted that he had not yet received this manifestation. Nevertheless, he proclaimed it as God's Word.

Seymour's sermon was met with mixed reactions. While some agreed with him favorably, others denounced him fervently. A family by the name of Lee invited him home for Sunday dinner. When returning with him to the mission that evening, they found that Sister Hutchinson had padlocked the doors. She was outraged and declared that she wouldn't permit such extreme teaching in her little mission on Santa Fe Street. And Seymour was denied access to his mission sleeping room.[8]

Seymour now found himself with little money and no place to stay. So the Lees felt obligated to take him home… although they did have reservations. While staying with the Lees, Seymour remained behind the closed doors of his room in prayer and fasting. Then after many days, he invited the Lees to pray with him. They accepted his invitation, and began to feel differently toward him. Soon other members of the mission heard of the prayer meetings at the Lee household. They began gathering there and Seymour became known as a man of prayer.[9]

When Sister Hutchinson learned of those who were joining Seymour, she arranged a meeting between Seymour and the Holiness clergy to determine the origin of the error. Seymour faced a large, difficult audience of Holiness preachers in his inquisition, but he clung to the Word. He read again from Acts 2:4 and explained that unless the Holiness preachers had the experience that took place in the Upper Room, they weren't baptized in the Holy Spirit. According to Seymour, their problem was with the Word of God, not with him.

One minister who had been against Seymour would later say:

The contention was on our part. I have never met a man who had such control over his spirit. No amount of confusion and accusation seemed to disturb him. He would sit behind that packing case and smile at us until we were all condemned by our own activities.[10]

214 NORTH BONNIE BRAE STREET

William Seymour's calming leadership was noticed by all. Following the investigation into his teachings, the Asberys asked him to move into their home on North Bonnie Brae Street and begin holding regular meetings there. Seymour accepted, and the small group began to meet in late February 1906. Their meetings consisted of hours of prayer as they sought for the baptism of the Holy Spirit.

As the meetings grew, Seymour asked for the assistance of his longtime friend, Lucy Farrow. He explained to the group that Farrow had an extraordinary ability to present the baptism of the Holy Spirit, and so money was collected to bring her from Houston.

When Sister Farrow arrived, Seymour announced that the group would enter into a ten-day fast until they received the divine blessing of the baptism of the Holy Spirit. The group fasted and prayed through the weekend. Then on Monday, Mr. Lee called Seymour to his home to ask for the prayer of healing. Seymour anointed Lee with oil, prayed for him, and Lee was healed instantly. Then Lee asked Seymour to lay hands on him and pray for the baptism of the Holy Spirit. So Seymour

The home of Mr. and Mrs. Richard Asbery on North Bonnie Brae Street.

An undated photo of the Asbery home site memorializes it as the birthplace
of the Pentecostal movement.

laid hands on him again, and this time, Lee broke out speaking loudly in other tongues! The two rejoiced ecstatically for the rest of the day, then walked together to the evening prayer meeting.

When they arrived at the Asbery home on Bonnie Brae Street, every room was packed with people. Many were already praying. Seymour took charge of the meeting, leading the group in songs, testimonies, and more prayer. Then, he began to tell the story of Mr. Lee's healing and his infilling of the Holy Spirit. As soon as Seymour finished, Lee raised his hands and began to speak in other tongues. The entire group dropped to their knees as they worshiped God and cried out for the baptism. Then, six or seven people lifted their voices and began to speak in another tongue. Jennie Evans Moore, who would later marry Seymour, fell to her knees from the piano bench as one of the first to speak in tongues.

Some people rushed outside to the front porch, prophesying and preaching. Others, while speaking in tongues, ran into the streets for all the neighborhood to hear. The Asberys' young daughter rushed into the living room to see what was happening, only to meet her frightened brother running the other way! Then Jennie Evans Moore returned to the piano and began singing with her beautiful voice—in up to six languages—all with interpretation. The meeting lasted until well past ten o'clock that night, when everyone left in great joy and thankfulness.[11]

For three days, they celebrated what they called "early Pentecost restored." The news spread quickly, bringing crowds that filled the Asberys' yard and surrounded their home. Groups from every culture began to find their way to 214 North Bonnie

Brae Street. Some would stand outside the windows, hoping to hear someone pray in tongues. At times, they heard great shouting, while at other times, it was intensely quiet. Many fell "under the power" and lay on the floor—some for three to five hours.[12]

Unusual healings also took place. One person said:

> The noise of the great outpouring of the Spirit drew me. I had been nothing but a "walking drug store" all my life, with weak lungs and cancer. As they looked at me, they said, "Child, God will heal you." In those days of the great outpouring, when they said God would heal you, you were healed. For thirty-three years, I have never gone back to the doctors, thank God, nor any of that old medicine! The Lord saved me, baptized me with the Holy Ghost, healed me, and sent me on my way rejoicing.[13]

It is said that the Asberys' "front porch became the pulpit and the street the pews" as Seymour would address the people from this home. Eventually, the front porch collapsed because of the weight of the crowd, but it was quickly reinforced so the meetings could continue.

It was late during the third night of these meetings—on April 12, 1906—that Seymour finally experienced his own encounter with the Holy Spirit. After many had left, Seymour himself was filled and began to speak in other tongues. He was kneeling beside a man who was helping him pray for a breakthrough, when at last he received. The long-awaited gift of the

The Apostolic Faith Gospel Mission at 312 Azusa Street.
The sign at left hanging outside the second story reads,
"Ye Shall Know the Truth and the Truth Shall Make You Free… God is Love."

Holy Spirit had finally come to the man whose preaching had brought His freedom to so many others.

312 AZUSA STREET

Everyone knew another meeting place had to be found quickly. The Asbery home could no longer accommodate the crowds. So on April 14, 1906, Seymour and his elders set out to find the perfect place. They wandered around the city near their area, until they came upon a dead-end street that was about a half a mile long. It was there, in the industrial business section of Los Angeles, that Seymour found what had once been an old Methodist church. After its use by the Methodists, the building had been remodeled for a different purpose. It had been divided in half and the top section had been turned into apartments. But a fire had destroyed the floor and the cathedral-shaped roof had been flattened and covered with tar.

When Seymour acquired the building, the top floor was being used for storage, while the bottom floor had been converted into a horse stable. The windows were broken and bare electric light bulbs hung from the ceiling. Seymour was offered the building for eight dollars a month.[14]

As the word got out, people came from everywhere to help restore the building. A. G. Osterburg, the pastor of the local Full Gospel Church, paid several men to help renovate the building. Volunteers swept the floors and whitewashed the walls. J. V. McNeil, a devout Catholic and owner of the largest lumber company in Los Angeles, donated lumber for the cause.

Sawdust was placed on the floor, and planks were nailed to wooden barrels for use as pews. Two empty crates were nailed on top of each other to act as Seymour's pulpit.

It was in this humble, skid-row-like setting that the new tenants of 312 Azusa Street prepared themselves for international revival.

BEGINNING STAGES

The great San Francisco earthquake took place on April 18, 1906. The next day, a lesser shock was felt in Los Angeles. Out of fear, many repented of their sins. Hundreds of people fled to Azusa to hear the gospel message and experience the baptism in the Holy Spirit with the evidence of speaking in other tongues. Even the very wealthy came to this lower-class area to hear of God's power.

The seating arrangement at Azusa was unique. Because there was no platform, Seymour sat on the same level with the rest of the congregation. And the benches were arranged so the participants faced one another. The meetings were spontaneous, so no one ever knew what would happen or who the speaker would be.

In the beginning stages of Azusa, all of the music was impromptu, without the use of instruments or hymn books. The meetings began with someone singing a song or giving a testimony. Because there was no program, someone would finally rise, anointed to bring forth the message. The speaker could be any race, age, or gender. And everyone felt that God

William Seymour, seated second from right, is surrounded by the
Azusa Street Revival team of ministers.
His future wife, Jennie, is standing third from left.

was responsible for the altar calls, which could take place at any point during the meetings.

At Azusa Street, sermons were inspired in English or in tongues with interpretation. Sometimes the services ran continuously for ten to twelve hours. Sometimes they ran for several days and nights! Many said the congregation never tired because they were so energized by the Holy Spirit. After the services ended in the early morning hours, many could be seen congregating under the streetlights, talking about the Lord.

At Azusa, the services were so anointed that if anyone got up to speak from their intellectual understanding, the Spirit-filled believers would break out in wailing sobs. This has been well-illustrated in a story about a woman called Mother Jones. One man rose to speak, apparently not being led by the Spirit. As he stood and preached, Mother Jones is said to have quietly hurried up to the platform, where she sat at the foot of the pulpit and stared up at the fellow with icy, foreboding eyes. Finally, she said, "Can't you see that you aren't anointed to preach?" Because of this incident, Mother Jones quickly earned a reputation that discouraged any unanointed preacher from standing at the pulpit. It is said that all she had to do was stand up and the unanointed preacher would run from the pulpit!

Soon, all classes of people began attending the Azusa Street meetings. In his book *Azusa Street*, Frank Bartleman wrote:

Many were curious and unbelieving, but others were hungry for God. Outside persecution never hurt the

William Seymour reads his Bible.

work. We had to fear from the working of evil spirits within. Even spiritualists and hypnotists came to investigate, and to try their influence. Then all the religious sore-heads and crooks came, seeking a place in the work. But this is always the danger to every new work. They have no place elsewhere. This condition cast a fear over many which was hard to overcome. It hindered the Spirit much. Many were afraid to seek God, for fear the devil might get them.[15]

Bartleman also wrote:

We found early in the "Azusa" work that when we attempted to steady the Ark, the Lord stopped working. We dared not call the attention of the people too much to the working of the evil. Fear would follow. We could only pray. Then God gave the victory. There was a presence of God with us, through prayer, we could depend on. The leaders had limited experience, and the wonder is the work survived at all against its powerful adversaries.[16]

Bartleman's statement may be one of the main reasons that Seymour has been severely criticized as a leader. God was looking for a willing vessel—and He found it in Seymour. God was not looking for those who brag of their status and experience. However, in spiritual terms, Seymour's limited experience may have been the cause of his difficulties. Leadership should expound strongly on the truth instead of focusing on that which

The Azusa Street mission operated day and night.

is false; and deceit can't stand against the authority, strength, and wisdom of prayerful, godly leadership. In that regard, it is good that they depended on prayer. Prayer will see you through. But God also gives His leadership a voice. That voice, by the strength of the Holy Spirit, will know how to separate that which is of value from the counterfeit that will tarnish. Strong, godly leadership can separate the gold from the brass.

Despite some spiritual confusion, Azusa began operating day and night. The entire building had been organized for full use. Great emphasis had been placed on the blood of Jesus, inspiring the group to a higher standard of living. And divine love began to manifest, allowing no unkind words to be spoken of another. The people were careful to make sure that the Spirit of God wouldn't be grieved. Both the rich, educated people and the poor, unlearned people sat as one in the sawdust and make-shift barrel pews.

PACKING THE STREETS, FALLING LIKE TREES

One man at Azusa said:

I would have rather lived six months at that time than fifty years of ordinary life. I have stopped more than once within two blocks of the place and prayed for strength before I dared go on. The presence of the Lord was so real.[17]

It was said that the power of God could be felt at Azusa, even outside the building. Scores of people were seen dropping into a prostrate position in the streets before they ever reached the mission. Then many would rise, speaking in tongues without any assistance from those inside.[18]

By summer, crowds had reached staggering numbers, of ten into the thousands. The scene had become an international gathering. One account states:

> Every day trains unloaded numbers of visitors who came from all over the continent. News accounts of the meeting spread over the nation in both the secular and religious press.[19]

Inexperience may have been prevalent at the beginning, but seasoned veterans of ministry were now arriving to help support Seymour's work. Most came from the Holiness ranks, or were missionaries returning from the nations. The result of this seasoned mixture of people was a wonderful new host of missionaries who were dispatched around the world. Many, newly baptized in the Holy Spirit, would feel a call to a certain nation. So men and women were now departing for Scandinavia, China, India, Egypt, Ireland, and various other nations. Even Sister Hutchinson, who initially locked Seymour out of her mission, came to Azusa, received the baptism of the Holy Spirit, and left for Africa.[20]

Owen Adams of California traveled to Canada from Azusa, where he met Robert Semple, Aimee Semple McPherson's first husband. When Adams met Semple, he told him of the miraculous events at Azusa and of his experience of speaking in tongues. Semple then excitedly told his new bride, Aimee, before they went on to China, where Robert Semple would die. But Adam's news had birthed a burning curiosity in the heart of young Aimee. When she returned to America, she would make Los Angeles her base from where her phenomenal ministry would rise.[21]

Though there was much excitement swirling around about the baptism of the Holy Spirit at Azusa, many misunderstood the ultimate purpose of speaking in other tongues. Many felt it was only a divine language for the nation to which they were sent.[22]

At this time, everyone seemed to love William Seymour. When the Spirit moved, he was known to keep his head inside of the top box crate that sat in front of him, bowed in prayer. He never asked for a salary, so he would very often be seen "walking through the crowds with five and ten dollar bills sticking out of his hip pockets, which people had crammed there unnoticed by him."[23]

John G. Lake visited the Azusa Street meetings. In his book *Adventures With God*, he would later write of Seymour:

He had the funniest vocabulary. But I want to tell you, there were doctors, lawyers, and professors, listening to the marvelous things coming from his lips. It was not what he said in words, it was what he said from his spirit to my heart that showed me he had more of God in his

William J. Seymour, seated at left, and John G. Lake, right,
are joined by other men associated with the Azusa Street revival.
Standing, from left, are John A. D. Adams, F. F. Bosworth, and Tom Hezmalhalch.

life than any man I had ever met up to that time. It was God in him that attracted the people.[24]

Missionaries were called from their nations to come and witness the spiritual phenomena in Los Angeles. Many came, then carried Azusa Street's Pentecostal message around the world. No one could possibly record all the miracles that occurred there.

The members of Azusa all carried tiny bottles of oil wherever they went. They would knock on doors to witness and pray for the sick throughout Los Angeles. They stood on street corners, singing and preaching, and worked as volunteers to clothe the poor and feed the hungry. It was exciting and incredible.

In September 1906, due to popular demand, Seymour began a publication entitled *The Apostolic Faith*. Within a few months, the mailing list grew to over twenty thousand names. By the next year, it had more than doubled. In this publication, Seymour announced his intention to restore "the faith once delivered" by old-time preaching, camp meetings, revivals, missions, and street and prison work.[25]

In the first publication, Seymour wrote, "Multitudes have come. God makes no difference in nationality."[26] Then, a few months later, he wrote:

The meeting has been a melting time. The people are all melted together…made one lump, one bread, all one body in Christ Jesus. There is no Jew or Gentile, bond or free, in the Azusa Mission. No instrument that God can use is rejected on account of color or dress or lack of education. This is why God has built up the work.... The sweetest thing is the loving harmony.[27]

Obviously, these were revolutionary words in a time of such racial division.

BEGINNINGS OF DECLINE

Persecution outside of Azusa was expected, but it finally began within. Early one autumn morning, some members arrived at the mission to see the words "Apostolic Faith Mission" written across the top of the building, and started accusing the mission of evolving into just another denomination. This was the name of Seymour's early mentor's movement, so the Azusa Mission was now being perceived as a loose offshoot of Charles Parham's ministry. And many feared the mission was becoming just another in Parham's network of churches and Bible schools.

One who was there wrote:

From that time, the trouble and division began. It was no longer a free Spirit for all as it had been. The work had become one more rival party and body, along with the other churches and sects of the city... the church is an organism, not a human organization.[28]

By now, Azusa outreach centers had been planted in Seattle and Portland under the direction of a woman by the name of Florence Crawford. And the Los Angeles headquarters was attempting to draw the entire West Coast revival outlets into their organization, but failed. So the revival itself was slowly setting itself up for ultimate failure.

"TARRYING" AND TONGUES

The new body of believers also had a misconception about the "tarrying" concept. They would simply wait for hours for the Spirit to come, and restlessness began to surface when they felt many were abusing this time. What they didn't realize was that the Holy Spirit had already come. He was there!

Then there was the confusion surrounding their understanding of speaking in other tongues. Up to this point, it had primarily been taught that tongues were for foreign missions. They believed that if a person were to go to the mission field, they would be gifted to preach in the nation's language. Many Azusa missionaries were greatly disappointed when they discovered this was not the rule. Though it is a biblical and historical fact that tongues will manifest for that purpose, this is not their only use! It would be later, during the growth of the Pentecostal movement, that tongues would be understood as a prayer language as well. But at Azusa Street, the experience of speaking in tongues was in its "first diaper"!

Azusa members also believed that a person only needed to speak in tongues once to be filled with the Holy Spirit. To the early Azusa members, speaking in other tongues was a sovereign move of God that meant waiting for God to come upon them.

Along with these misunderstandings, accusations of fleshly manifestations that people called the moving of the Holy Spirit began circulating. With this spiritual understanding being so new, can you imagine how it must have been to lead it? It was here that Seymour wrote to Charles Parham, and asked him to come to Azusa to hold a general revival.

FANATICS, FAKES, AND FRACTION

Though Seymour didn't fully agree with all of Parham's theology, I believe he respected and trusted Parham's leadership experience. Perhaps he felt Parham could present another view and ignite a fresh move of God.

It is said that many others had written letters to Parham begging him to come and determine which manifestations at Azusa were counterfeit and which were real. While there is not documentation of these letters, Mrs. Pauline Parham has claimed that some are in her collections.[29] We do have one letter written by Seymour to Parham that states:

> We are expecting a general one [revival] to start again when you come, that these little revivals will all come together and make one great union revival.[30]

It is true that there were many divisions within the Los Angeles revival. But by previous examples of Seymour's character, I believe he wanted Parham to unite the city instead of disciplining it. And it is certain that Parham wouldn't have come to Azusa without an invitation.

When Parham arrived, Seymour introduced him as the "father in this gospel of the kingdom."[31] We believe Seymour was sincere. He needed a spiritual father to help him lead this great movement. But whatever he had expected from Parham, things didn't go as Seymour had planned. After Parham's sermons and private exhortations, Seymour padlocked the mission's door to keep Parham out.

What did Parham say to Seymour? What could have caused him to lock Parham out of Azusa? While it is true that Parham's background in education, leadership, and experience differed from Seymour's, their views on the baptism of the Holy Spirit seemed to be the same.

Or were they?

Parham sat in the service while looking on in horror at the manifestations around him. In Parham's services, a certain liberality was allowed, but nothing that bordered on fanaticism. Some of Parham's own Bible school students even felt he was too strict in his definition of "fanaticism." And at Azusa, besides the shouting and dancing, the people jerked and shook. It was a highly emotional atmosphere, and there were many genuine, Spirit-filled expressions along with the false. Because of the many cultures represented, Seymour believed that each person should allow their own emotional experience, based on how each individual understood the moving of the Spirit, whether it was right or wrong.

Seymour's theology was to allow the Holy Spirit to do whatever He wanted. But only a few knew enough about the movings of the Spirit to lead the people in it. Seymour felt that if a culture was forced into a certain mode or expression, the Holy Spirit wouldn't manifest Himself among them. There is some sense that Seymour was spiritually sensitive in his leadership, and followed this to the best of his ability. There is a fine line between wounding the human spirit and offending the Holy Spirit.

There is no known written account from Seymour regarding certain hypnotism accounts. But there are from Parham. Here is his account:

> I hurried to Los Angeles, and to my utter surprise and astonishment I found conditions even worse than I had anticipated...manifestations of the flesh, spiritualistic controls, saw people practicing hypnotism at the altar over candidates seeking baptism, though many were receiving the real baptism of the Holy Ghost.
>
> After preaching two or three times, I was informed by two of the elders that I was not wanted in that place. With workers from Texas, we opened a great revival in the W.C.T.U. Building in Los Angeles. Great numbers were saved, marvelous healings took place, and between two and three hundred who had been possessed of awful fits and spasms and controls in the Azusa Street work were delivered, and received the real Pentecost teachings and spake with other tongues.
>
> In speaking of different phases of fanaticism that have been obtained here, that I do so with all loving

kindness and at the same time with all fairness and firmness. Let me speak plainly with regard to the work as I have found it here. I found hypnotic influences, familiar-spirit influences, spiritualistic influences, mesmeric influences, and all kinds of spells, spasms, falling in trances, etc.

A word about the baptism of the Holy Ghost. The speaking in tongues is never brought about by any of the above practices/influences. No such thing is known among our workers as the suggestion of certain words and sounds, the working of the chin, or the massage of the throat. There are many in Los Angeles who sing, pray and talk wonderfully in other tongues, as the Spirit gives utterance, and there is jabbering here that is not tongues at all. The Holy Ghost does nothing that is unnatural or unseemly, and any strained exertion of body, mind or voice is not the work of the Holy Spirit, but of some familiar spirit, or other influence. The Holy Ghost never leads us beyond the point of self-control or the control of others, while familiar spirits or fanaticism lead us both beyond self-control and the power to help others.[32]

Perhaps Parham's perception was right; still, the results may have been different if Parham had been more fatherly than dictatorial. Seymour never changed his theology and neither did Parham. Seymour wouldn't mention the rivalry for some two months. And even when he finally did, his account was discreet, avoiding any direct criticism. Seymour wrote:

Some are asking if Dr. Charles F. Parham is the leader of this movement. We can answer, no he is not the leader of this movement of Azusa Mission. We thought of having him to be our leader and so stated in our paper, before waiting on the Lord. We can be rather hasty, especially when we are very young in the power of the Holy Spirit. We are just like a baby—full of love—and were willing to accept anyone that had the baptism with the Holy Spirit as our leader. But the Lord commenced settling us down, and we saw that the Lord should be our leader. So we honor Jesus as the Great Shepherd of the sheep. He is our model.[33]

So in attempting to uphold his doctrine of unity, Seymour remained true to his teachings by not allowing an unkind word to be spoken against any of his accusers.

THE SANCTIFICATION SLUR

Though Seymour followed John Wesley, he didn't follow his teachings on sanctification. Seymour believed one could lose their salvation if they reacted in the flesh. He taught that sanctification, or sinless perfection, was a separate work of grace aside from salvation. Once you were sanctified, Seymour believed, you acted sanctified all the time. But if you sinned, you lost it.

Can you imagine the trouble and accusations that kind of teaching caused within Azusa? Many overzealous believers got caught up in pointing fingers and judging one another. Their self-righteous behavior resulted in clashes, splits, and controversies. In fact, this is one of the main reasons Seymour never reacted in the flesh to any persecution that came against him. According to his theology, this was necessary to keep his salvation. He said:

> If you get angry, or speak evil, or backbite, I care not how many tongues you may have, you have not the baptism with the Holy Spirit. You have lost your salvation.[34]

Seymour would padlock an opposing minister, but he would never speak out against him!

LOVE AND BETRAYAL

In spite of the many accusations, mistakes, and persecutions, Seymour remained faithful in his purpose for revival. It seemed he trusted and believed the best of almost everyone. True to his gentle, almost naive nature, he would later write:

> You cannot win people by preaching against their church or pastor…if you get to preaching against churches, you will find that sweet Spirit of Christ…is lacking and a harsh judging spirit takes place. The churches are not to be blamed for divisions. People were hunting for light. They built up denominations because they did not know a better way. When people run out of the love of God, they get to preaching dress, and meats, and doctrines of men and preaching against churches. All these denominations are our brethren…. So let us seek peace and not

William J. Seymour and his lovely wife, Jennie.

confusion…. The moment we feel we have all the truth or more than anyone else, we will drop.[35]

The next spring, Seymour had to decide whether he would purchase Azusa or move to another location. So he presented the option to the congregation and they agreed to make an immediate payment of $4,000 toward the $15,000 needed. Within a year, the remaining balance was paid, far ahead of schedule. By this time, reports of miracles and newly-founded missions poured into Los Angeles from all over the world. Encouraged, Seymour commented, "We are on the verge of the greatest miracle the world has ever seen."[36]

During this time, Seymour's thoughts turned to marriage. Jennie Evans Moore, a faithful member of his ministry in Los Angeles, became his wife. She was known for her beauty, musical talents, and spiritual sensitivity. She was a very gentle woman and was always faithful to stand beside Seymour. It was Jennie who felt the Lord would have them marry, and Seymour agreed. So the couple married on May 13, 1908. After the ceremony, William and Jennie moved into a modest apartment upstairs in the Azusa Mission.

But the news of their marriage angered a small yet very influential group at the Mission. One of the main antagonists was Clara Lum, the mission's secretary responsible for the newspaper's publication. After learning of Seymour's marriage, she abruptly decided that it was time to leave the mission.

A few believers at Azusa had some very odd ideas about marriage. Lum's group believed marriage in the last days to be a disgrace because of the soon return of Christ and severely denounced Seymour for his decision.

It may have been that Clara Lum was secretly in love with Seymour, and left because of her jealousy. Whatever the reason, she relocated to Portland, Oregon, to join the mission headed by a former Azusa associate, Florence Crawford. And when she did, she took the entire national and international mailing lists with her.

This unthinkable action crippled Seymour's worldwide publication outreach. His entire national and international lists of over fifty thousand names had been stolen, leaving him with only their Los Angeles list. Then when the May 1908 *Apostolic Faith* was sent out, the cover looked the same, but inside was a column announcing its new address in Portland for contributions and mail. The thousands who eagerly read and sent contributions to the newspaper now started sending them to Portland without questioning the change. By the June issue, no article by Seymour appeared at all. Finally, by midsummer of 1908, all references to Los Angeles were omitted entirely. When it became clear that Lum wouldn't be returning, the Seymours traveled to Portland to confront Lum and ask for the lists. But the lists were never returned. Without this vital information, it was impossible for Seymour to continue the publication, and thus ended a dramatic era of Azusa.

THE LAST DIVISION: MAN OR GOD?

Throughout 1909 and 1910, Seymour continued his ministry at Azusa, though the number of people decreased dramatically due to lack of influence and funds. So he left two young men in charge at the mission and departed for Chicago on a cross-country preaching tour. In early 1911, William H. Durham held meetings at Azusa in his place.

Durham's dramatic preaching caused hundreds to flock again to the mission. Many of the old Azusa workers from various parts of the world even returned to the mission. They called it "the second shower of the latter rain," as the fire began to fall at Azusa once again. In one service, over five hundred people had to be turned away. So between the services, the people wouldn't leave their seats for fear of losing them.[37]

The last conflict at Azusa took place between Seymour and Durham. The two differed greatly in their theology. Durham preached adamantly, and soundly, that people couldn't lose their salvation even if they sinned in the flesh. Salvation was by faith with works involved, not by works alone. Durham preached the needed balance between law and grace that the Pentecostal movement desperately needed because the "works" doctrine had led to many divisions.[38] His teaching felt like a cool rain on those who heard. It literally brought the people in droves!

Alarmed by Durham's large following and doctrinal differences, the elders of Azusa contacted Seymour. He returned immediately to Los Angeles for a conference. But Seymour and Durham couldn't come to an agreement in their doctrine. So in May, Seymour used the padlock again, locking Durham out of the mission![39]

Unshaken by this action, Durham and his workers secured a large, two-story building that seated more than one thousand people. The upstairs served as a prayer room, which was open day and night. The crowds from Azusa followed Durham. Thousands were saved, baptized, and healed while the old Azusa Mission became virtually deserted.

"TIRED AND WORN"

But the old Azusa Mission remained open to anyone who would come. Seymour remained its leader and kept his doctrine the same, though no one seemed interested in attending. He changed Azusa's meeting schedule to one all-day service to be held on Sunday. And he regularly attempted to increase the meetings, but the interest was not there. In the end, only twenty people remained, and they were mainly those from the original Azusa group. At times, visitors came from the previous "glory days," and of course Seymour was elated in welcoming them. But he spent more and more time reading and reflecting.

In 1921, William Seymour made his last ministry campaign across America. When he returned to Los Angeles in 1922, people began to notice that he looked very weary. He attended many ministry conventions, but was never publicly recognized from the platform.

Finally on September 28, 1922, while at the mission, Seymour suffered a sudden attack of severe pain in his chest. One of the workers ran for the doctor who was only blocks away. Upon examination, Seymour was told to rest. Then at

5:00 p.m. that same afternoon, while he was dictating a letter, another chest pain clinched him. He struggled for breath, then went to be with the Lord at the age of fifty-two. The cause of his death was officially cited as heart failure.

The revivalist was buried in a simple redwood casket at Evergreen Cemetery in Los Angeles. He was appropriately laid to rest amid the graves of others from many nations and continents. The words on his tombstone simply read, "Our Pastor." Sadly, only two hundred people attended William Seymour's funeral, but they gave many testimonies of God's greatness through this frontline general's ministry.

SHADOWS AND WOLVES

Following the years after Seymour's death, Mrs. Seymour carried on as pastor of the Azusa Street Mission. Everything continued smoothly for eight years. Then more problems arose in 1931. Through a series of legal battles waged by someone trying to take over the mission, city officials became annoyed with the group and declared the property a fire hazard. Later that year, it was demolished, but not before it was offered to a Pentecostal denomination who replied, "We are not interested in relics."[40] Today only a street sign stands over the property, which is now nothing more than a vacant lot.

Five years later, Mrs. Seymour was admitted to the county hospital for terminal care. Jennie died of heart failure and joined her husband in heaven on July 2, 1936.

William Seymour's gravesite and memorial plaque.

THE LEGACY OF POWER

Though the legacy and ministry of William J. Seymour seems heartbreaking, the results of his efforts between 1906 and 1909 produced and exploded the Pentecostal movement around the world. Today, many denominations attribute their founding to the participants of Azusa. Most of the early Assembly of God leaders came out of Azusa. Demos Shakarian, founder of the Full Gospel Businessmen's Fellowship, said his grandfather was an original Azusa member. The evangelistic efforts of the Valdez family, the Garr family, Dr. Charles Price, and countless others are also linked to this revival.

Probably everyone in the Pentecostal movement today can attribute their roots, in some way, to Azusa. Regardless of all the controversy and Azusa's peculiar doctrines, whenever Azusa is mentioned, most immediately think of the power of the Holy Spirit that was poured on their ranks.

GOD IS NOT A RACIST

Some have tried to make the Azusa Street Revival and the ministry of Seymour a racial issue. Unfortunately, sometimes a pure move of God gets hidden under racial overtones. Perhaps this is one of the main reasons Azusa lasted for only three short years. God won't allow His glory to fall prey to the arguments of men. If that should happen, He leaves—end of discussion.

Some who seem racially influenced get upset that Seymour is called the "catalyst" of Pentecost instead of the "father" of it. According to *Webster's Dictionary*, a "catalyst" is something that "precipitates a process or event, and increases the rate at which a reaction takes place." That is exactly what Seymour did. William Seymour's Pentecostal ministry increased public awareness to such a degree that it not only turned around a major U.S. city, it also spread throughout the world at an incredible pace. It seems that every continent was touched in some way by the revival at Azusa.

As was mentioned earlier, racial issues were only a small part of the many interferences that visited Azusa. A potentially greater error is made when this revival is looked upon as primarily a black-and-white issue. No particular race can claim the patent on a move of God. God has never worked according to the color of man; He operates through the heart of man.

As we continue to explore the great generals of our past and determine to learn from their successes, don't allow yourself to be counted among their failures. Refuse to listen to the voices of yesterday and today who only see appearances. Rather, follow those who press into God's Spirit. Let us go on to maturity and fight for the prize rather than personal glory.

Only eternity will fully reveal the fruit of William J. Seymour's ministry. One thing is clear: he was an able stick of dynamite who God could use to send the explosions of Pentecostal revival around the world. And He did.

A street sign shows where the Azusa Street Mission stood during the revival.

A 1956 sign in Los Angeles announces services to celebrate the golden anniversary
of the Azusa Street Revival.

ENDNOTES

1. A. C. Valdez Sr., *Fire on Azusa Street* (Costa Mesa, CA: Gift Publications, 1980), 87-89.

2. Emma Cotton, *Personal Reminiscences* (Los Angeles, CA: West Coast Publishers, 1930), 2, quoted in "Inside Story of the Outpouring of the Holy Spirit, Azusa Street, April 1906," published in *Message of the Apostolic Faith*, April 1939, Vol. 1, 1-3.

3. James S. Tinney, *In the Tradition of William J. Seymour*, 13, quoted from "Father of Modern Day Pentecostalism," in *Journal of the Interdenominational Theological Center*, 4 (Fall 1976),
34-44, and taken from Dr. Duane Miller, Autobiography.

4. Mrs. Charles Parham, *The Life of Charles F. Parham* (Birminham: Commercial Printing Co., 1930), 112-123.

5. Ibid., Tinney, *In the Tradition of William J. Seymour*, 14.

6. Ibid., 15.

7. Frank Bartleman, *Azusa Street* (Plainfield, NJ: Logos International, 1980), 33, 90.

8. C. W. Shrunway, *A Critical Study of the Gift of Tongues*, A. B. dissertation, University of California, July 1914, 173, and *A Critical History of Glossolalia*, Ph.D. thesis, Boston University, 1919.

9. Cotton, *Personal Reminiscences*, 2.

10. C. M. McGowan, *Another Echo From Azusa* (Covina, CA: Oak View Christian Home), 3.

11. Thomas Nickel, *Azusa Street Outpouring* (Hanford, CA: Great Commission International, 1956, 1979, 1986), 5, and Shumway, *A Critical Study of the Gift of Tongues*, 175.

12. Shumway, *A Critical Study of the Gift of Tongues*, 175-176, and Cotton, *Personal Reminiscences*, 2.

13. Cotton, *Personal Reminiscences*, 3.

14. Shumway, *A Critical Study of the Gift of Tongues*, 175-176.

15. Bartleman, *Azusa Street*, 48.

16. Ibid.

17. Ibid., 59-60.

18. Tinney, *In the Tradition of William J. Seymour*, 17.

19. Ibid.

20. Nickel, *Azusa Street Outpouring*, 18.

21. Ibid.

22. Shumway, *A Critical Study of the Gift of Tongues*, 44-45.

23. Tinney, *In the Tradition of William J. Seymour*, 18.
24. John G. Lake, *Adventures in God* (Tulsa, OK: Harrison House, Inc., 1981), 18-19.
25. Ibid., 18.
26. *Apostolic Faith*, September 1906.
27. Ibid., November and December 1906.
28. Bartleman, *Azusa Street*, 68-69.
29. Interview with Mrs. Pauline Parham.
30. Parham, *The Life of Charles F. Parham*, 154.
31. Ibid., 163.
32. Ibid., 163-170.
33. *Apostolic Faith*, December 1906.
34. Ibid., June 1907.
35. Ibid., January 1907.
36. Ibid., October 1907-January 1908.
37. Bartleman, *Azusa Street*, 150.
38. Ibid., 150-151, and Valdez, *Fire on Azusa Street*, 26.
39. Bartleman, *Azusa Street*, 151.
40. Tinney, *In the Tradition of William J. Seymour*, 19.

William J. Seymour

PART TWO

SERMONS AND WRITINGS OF
WILLIAM J. SEYMOUR

INTRODUCTION

Roberts Liardon

William Seymour was not a wild-eyed flamboyant black Pentecostal preacher. He was a meek man with a direct style that was not often dynamic in presentation; he could, however, become suddenly and volcanically emotional at times, in and out of the pulpit. He saw himself more as a teacher than a preacher, and as you read his sermons, you will be impressed with the depth of his insights into the work of Christ and the Holy Spirit.

The Azusa Street meetings were long, and on the whole, they were spontaneous. In its early days, music was generally without instruments, although one or two instruments were included at times. Jennie Evans Moore would sometimes play the piano during worship. There were songs, testimonies given by visitors or read from those who sent letters of testimonies to the mission, prayer, and altar calls for salvation, sanctification, or baptism in the Holy Spirit. And there was preaching. Sermons were generally not prepared in advance but were typically spontaneous.

The meetings at the Apostolic Faith Mission quickly caught the attention of the press due to the dynamic nature of the worship. Between 300 and 350 people could get into the whitewashed 40-by-60-foot wood frame structure, with many others occasionally forced to stand outside. Church services were held on the first floor, where the benches were placed in a rectangular pattern. Some of the benches were simply planks put on top of empty nail kegs. There was no elevated platform. There was no pulpit at the beginning of the revival.

In the *Los Angeles Times*, Arthur Osterburg, one of the key persons at the revival, described Brother Seymour with these words:

> He was meek and plain spoken and no orator. He spoke the common language of the uneducated class. He might preach for three-quarters of an hour with no more emotionalism than that post. He was no arm-waving thunderer, by any stretch of the imagination. The only way to explain the results is this: that his teachings were so simple that people who were opposed to

organized religion fell for it. It was the simplicity that attracted them.[1]

In September 1906, the first issue of the *Apostolic Faith* newspaper was printed and distributed at no cost. Florence Crawford, with the help of secretary Clara Lum and others, began putting the record of what was being said in the meetings into a newspaper format, under the supervision of William Seymour. In that first issue are descriptions of the revival, testimonies of healing and deliverance, and a note from Brother Parham, a listing of their doctrinal beliefs, a description of Seymour's call, and then the recording of William Seymour's first sermon, "The Precious Atonement."

There are teachings throughout the different issues that are not attributed to any particular author. In the thirteen issues of *The Apostolic Faith* newspapers, there are twenty sermons that are directly attributed to Brother Seymour—either his initials or name was written at the end of those messages. The following chapters are a collection of these sermons. They have not been changed substantially, only slightly edited for readability. Where Seymour quoted Scripture but did not give the citation, it has been included.

1 Robert Owens, *Speak to the Rock* (Lanham, MD: University Press of America, 1998), 57.

ONE

THE PRECIOUS ATONEMENT

Children of God, partakers of the precious atonement, let us study and see what there is in it for us.

First, through the atonement, we receive forgiveness of sins.

Second, we receive sanctification through the blood of Jesus. *"Wherefore Jesus also, that he might sanctify the people with his own blood, suffered without the gate"* (Hebrews 13:12).

Sanctified from all original sin, we become sons of God. "For both He that sanctifies and they who are sanctified are all of one: for which cause He is not ashamed to call them brethren." (See Hebrews 2:11.) (It seems that Jesus would be ashamed to call them brethren, if they were not sanctified.) Then you will not be ashamed to tell men and demons that you are sanctified, and are living a pure and holy life free from sin, a life that gives you power over the world, the flesh, and the devil. The devil does not like that kind of testimony. Through this precious atonement, we have freedom from all sin, though we are living in this world. We are permitted to sit in heavenly places in Christ Jesus.

Third, healing of our bodies. Sickness and disease are destroyed through the precious atonement of Jesus. How we ought to honor the stripes of Jesus, for "with His stripes we are healed." (See Isaiah 53:5.) How we ought to honor that precious body which the Father sanctified and sent into the world, not simply set apart, but really sanctified, soul, body, and spirit, free from sickness, disease, and everything of the devil. A body that knew no sin and disease was given for these imperfect bodies of ours. Not only is the atonement for the sanctification of our souls, but also for the sanctification of our bodies from inherited disease. It matters not what has been in the blood. Every drop of blood we received from our mother is impure. Sickness is born in a child just as original sin is born in the child. He was manifested to destroy the works of the devil. (See 1 John 3:8.) Every sickness is of the devil.

Man in the Garden of Eden was pure and happy and knew no sickness till that unholy visitor came into the garden, then his whole system was poisoned. It has been flowing in the blood of all the human family down the ages till God spoke to His people and said, *"I am the* LORD *that healeth thee"* (Exodus 15:26). The children of Israel practiced divine healing. David, after being healed of rheumatism (perhaps contracted in the caves where he hid himself from his pursuers), testified saying, *"Bless the* LORD, *O my soul: and all that is within me, bless his holy name…who forgiveth all thine iniquities; who healeth all thy diseases"* (Psalm 103:1, 3). David knew what it was to be healed. Healing continued with God's people till Solomon's heart was turned away by strange wives, and he brought in the black arts and mediums, and they went whoring after familiar spirits. God had been their healer, but after they lost the Spirit, they turned to the arm of flesh to find something to heal their diseases.

Thank God, we have a living Christ among us to heal our diseases. He will heal every case. The prophet had said, "With His stripes we are healed," and it was fulfilled when Jesus came. Also *"he hath borne our griefs"* (Isaiah 53:4), which means sickness, as translators tell us. Now if Jesus bore our sicknesses, why should we bear them? So, we get full salvation through the atonement of Jesus.

Fourth, we get the baptism with the Holy Ghost and fire upon the sanctified life. We get Christ enthroned and crowned in our hearts. Let us lift up Christ to the world in all His fullness, not only in healing and salvation from all sin, but in His power to speak all the languages of the world. We need the triune God to enable us to do this.

We that are the messengers of this precious atonement ought to preach all of it: justification, sanctification, healing, the baptism with the Holy Spirit, and signs following. *"How shall we escape, if we neglect so great salvation"* (Hebrews 2:3)? God is now confirming His Word by granting signs and wonders to follow the preaching of the full gospel in Los Angeles.

W. J. SEYMOUR
Vol. 1, No. 1

TWO

THE WAY INTO THE HOLIEST

A sinner comes to the Lord all wrapped up in sin and darkness. He cannot make any consecration because he is dead. The life has to be put into us before we can present our life to the Lord. He must get justified by faith. There is a Lamb without spot and blemish slain before God for him, and when he repents toward God for his sins, the Lord has mercy on him for Christ's sake, and put eternal life in his soul, pardoning him of his sins, washing away his guilty pollution, and he stands before God justified as if he had never sinned.

Then there remains that old original sin in him for which he is not responsible till he has the light. He hears that Jesus, *"that he might sanctify the people with his own blood, suffered without the gate"* (Hebrews 13:12), and he comes to be sanctified. There is Jesus, the Lamb without blemish, on the altar. Jesus takes that soul that has eternal life in it and presents it to God for thorough purging and cleansing from all original and Adamic sin. And Jesus, the Son of God, cleanses him from all sin, and he is made every whit whole, sanctified, and holy.

Now he is on the altar ready for the fire of God to fall, which is the baptism with the Holy Ghost. It is a free gift upon the sanctified, cleansed heart. The fire remains there continually burning in the Holiness of God. Why? Because he is sanctified and holy and on the altar continually. He stays there and the great Shekinah of glory is continually burning and filling with heavenly light.

W. J. SEYMOUR
Vol. l, No. 2

THREE

RIVER OF LIVING WATER

In the fourth chapter of John, the words come, *"Jesus answered and said unto her, If thou knewest the gift of God, and who it is that saith to thee, Give me to drink; thou wouldest have asked of him and he would have given thee living water"* (John 4:10). Praise God for the living waters today that flow freely, for they come from God to every hungry and thirsty heart.

Jesus said, "He that believeth on Me, as the Scripture hath said, out of his inmost being shall flow rivers of living waters." (See John 7:38.) Then we are able to go in the mighty name of Jesus to the ends of the earth and water dry places, deserts, and solitary places, until these parched, sad, lonely hearts are made to rejoice in the God of their salvation. We want the rivers today. Hallelujah! Glory to God in the highest!

In Jesus Christ, we get forgiveness of sin, and we get sanctification of our spirit, soul, and body, and upon that we get the gift of the Holy Ghost that Jesus promised to His disciples, the promise of the Father. All this we get through the atonement. Hallelujah!

The prophet said that he had borne our grief and sorrows. He was wounded for our transgressions, bruised for our iniquities, the chastisement of our peace was upon Him and with His stripes, we are healed. (See Isaiah 53:4–5.) So we get healing, health, salvation, joy, life—everything in Jesus. Glory to God! There are many wells today, but they are dry. There are many hungry souls today that are empty. But let us come to Jesus and take Him at His word and we will find wells of salvation, and be able to draw waters out of the well of salvation, for Jesus is that well.

At this time, Jesus was weary from a long journey. He sat on the well in Samaria, and a woman came to draw water. He asked her for a drink. She answered, *"How is it that thou, being a Jew, askest drink of me, which am a woman of Samaria? for the Jews have no dealings with the Samaritans"* (John 4:9). Jesus said, *"If thou knewest the gift of God, and who it is that saith to thee, Give me to drink; thou wouldest have asked of him, and he would have given thee living water"* (verse 10).

Oh, how sweet it was to see Jesus, the Lamb of God that takes away the sin of the world, that great sacrifice that God had given to a lost, dying, and benighted world, sitting on the well and talking with the woman. So gentle, so meek, and so kind that it gave her an appetite to talk further with Him, until He got into her secret and uncovered her life. Then she was pricked in heart, confessed her sins, and received pardon, cleansing from fornication and adultery, was washed from stain and guilt of sin and was made a child of God, and above all, received the well of salvation in her heart. It was so sweet and joyful, and good. Her heart was so filled with love that she felt she could take in a whole lost world. So she ran away with a well of salvation and left the old water pot on the well. How true it is in this day, when we get the baptism of the Holy Spirit, we have something to tell, and it is that the blood of Jesus Christ cleanses from all sin. The baptism with the Holy Ghost gives us power to testify to a risen resurrected Savior. Our affections are in Jesus Christ, the Lamb of God that takes away the sin of the world. How I worship Him today! How I praise Him for the all cleansing blood!

Jesus's promises are true and sure. The woman said to Him, after He had uncovered her secret, *"Sir, I perceive that thou art a prophet"* (John 4:19). Yes, He was a prophet. He was that great prophet that Moses said the Lord would raise up. He is here today. Will we be taught of that prophet? Will we hear Him? Let us accept Him in all His fullness.

He said, *"He that believeth on me, the works that I do shall he do also; and greater works than these shall he do; because I go unto my Father"* (John 14:12). These disciples to whom He was speaking had been saved, sanctified, and anointed with the Holy Spirit, their hearts had been opened to understand the Scriptures, and yet Jesus said, *"Tarry ye in the city of Jerusalem, until ye be endued with power from on high"* (Luke 24:49), and *"John truly baptized with water; but ye shall be baptized with the Holy Ghost not many days hence"* (Acts 1:5).

So the same commission comes to us. We find that they obeyed His commission and were all filled with the Holy Ghost on the day of Pentecost. Standing up, Peter said, *"This is that which was spoken by the prophet Joel"* (Acts 2:16). Dear loved ones; we preach the same sermon:

"This is that which was spoken by the prophet Joel; and it shall come to pass in the last days, saith God, I will pour out of my Spirit upon all flesh: and your sons and your daughters shall prophesy, and your young men shall see visions, and your old men shall dream dreams: and on my servants and on my handmaidens I will pour out in those days of my Spirit; and they shall prophesy.... For the promise is unto you, and to your children, and to all that are afar off, even as many as the Lord *our God shall call"* (Acts 2:16–18, 39). That means until now and to last until Jesus comes.

There are so many people today like the Samaritan woman at the well. They are controlled by the fathers. Our salvation is not in some father or human instrument. It is sad to see people so blinded, worshipping the creature more than the Creator. Listen to what the woman said, *"Our fathers worshipped in this mountain; and ye say, that in Jerusalem is the place where men ought to worship"* (John 4:20). So many people today are worshipping in the mountains, big churches, stone and frame buildings. But Jesus teaches that salvation is not in these stone structures—not in the mountains, not in the hills, but in God. For God is a Spirit. Jesus said unto her, *"Woman, believe me, the hour cometh* [and is], *when ye shall neither in this mountain, nor yet at Jerusalem, worship the Father"* (verse 21). So many people today are controlled by men. Their salvation reaches out no further than the boundary line of human creeds, but praise God for freedom in the Spirit. There are depths, heights, and breadths that we can reach through the power of the blessed Spirit. *"Eye hath not seen, nor ear heard, neither have entered into the heart of man, the things which God hath prepared for them that love him"* (1 Corinthians 2:9).

The Jews were the religious leaders at this time, and people had no more light upon salvation than the Jews gave them. The Jews were God's chosen people to evangelize the world. He had entrusted them to give all nations the true knowledge of God, but they went into traditions and doctrines of men, and were blinded and in the dark. Jesus came as the light of the world, and He is that light. *"If we walk in the light, as he is in the light, we have fellowship one with another, and the blood of Jesus Christ his Son cleanseth us from all sin"* (1 John 1:7).

Let us honor the Spirit, for Jesus has sent Him to teach and lead us into all truth. Above all, let us honor the blood of Jesus Christ every moment of our lives, and we will be sweet in our souls. We will be able to talk of this common salvation to everyone that we meet. God will let His anointing rest upon us in telling them of this precious truth. This truth belongs to God. We have no right to tax anyone for the truth, because God has entrusted us with it to tell it. Freely we receive, freely we give. So the gospel is to be preached freely, and God will bless it and spread it Himself, and we have experienced that He does. We have found Him true to His promise all the way. We have tried Him and proved Him. His promises are sure.

W. J. SEYMOUR
Vol. 1, No. 3

FOUR

IN MONEY MATTERS

There have been teachers who have told all the people to sell out, and many of them have gone into fanaticism. We let the Spirit lead people and tell them what they ought to give. When they get filled with the Spirit, their pocketbooks are converted and God makes them stewards and if He says, "Sell out," they will do so. But sometimes, they have families. God does not tell you to forsake your family. He says if you do not provide for your own, you are worse than an infidel. (See 1 Timothy 5:8.) Some are not called to go out and teach. We find some who have no wisdom nor faith, and the devil takes them to disgrace the work. Under false teaching, children have been left to go half naked, women have left their husbands, and husbands leave their wives to wash and scrub, and the Bible says that is worse than infidelity. Then they will go and borrow and cannot pay back. That person ought to go to work. The Bible says, *"Let him labour, working with his hands the thing which is good, that he may have to give to him that needeth"* (Ephesians 4:28).

Jesus sent those who were called out to preach the gospel to "take no thought what ye shall eat or drink." (See Matthew 6:25.) Get down and pray. Make your wants known unto God and He will send it in.

God does not expect all to sell out for He says, *"Now concerning the collection for the saints...upon the first day of the week let every one of you lay by him in store, as God hath prospered him"* (1 Corinthians 16:1–2). It does not mean for you to have great real estate and money banked up while your brothers and sisters are suffering. He means for you to turn loose because all that money is soon going to be thrown to the moles and bats. So it is better to spread the gospel and get stars in your crown than to be holding it. But for us to go and tell you to do it, pick out somebody who has money and read the Word to them, would not be the Spirit of the Lord. The Spirit will tell you what to do. When He wakes you up at night and tells you what to do, you cannot sleep till you obey. He says everyone shall be taught of God from the least to the greatest. (See Jeremiah 31:34; Hebrews 8:11.) God wants a free giver. (See 2 Corinthians 9:7.)

Ananias wanted to have a reputation that he sold out like the rest, so he plotted that he should give a portion and say he had sold out for the Lord. The Holy Ghost told Peter that Ananias had told a lie. (See Acts 5:1–5.) Peter told him the property was his. The Lord allows you to be the steward over it. The property was his and the sin was in lying to the Holy Ghost. It is right for you to have property, but if the Lord says, "Take $200, or $500, or $1,000, and distribute here or there," you do it. We must know our calling. We can work when baptized with the Holy Ghost. Some think they have got to preach. Well, we do preach in testifying. Some think they must go out because they have the tongues, but those are good for Los Angeles or anywhere else. The Lord will lead you by His small voice. (See 1 Kings 19:12.)

W. J. SEYMOUR
Vol. 1, No. 3

FIVE

COUNTERFEITS

God has told us in His precious Word that we should know a tree by its fruit. (See Luke 6:44.)

Wherever we find the real, we find the counterfeit also. But praise God for the real.

We find in the time of Peter, when men and women were receiving the power of the Holy Ghost, the counterfeit appeared in Ananias and Sapphira. But God's power was mightier than all the forces of hell, so their sin found them out. Be careful, dear loved ones, for your sin will surely find you out. *"But if we walk in the light, as he is in the light, we have fellowship one with another, and*

the blood of Jesus Christ his Son cleanseth us from all sin"
(1 John 1:7).

In our meetings, we have had people come and
claim that they had received the baptism with the Holy
Spirit, but when they were put to the test by the Holy
Spirit, they were found wanting. So they got down and
got saved and sanctified and baptized with the Holy
Spirit and spoke in tongues by the Holy Spirit. And
again people have imitated the gift of tongues, but how
quickly the Holy Spirit would reveal to every one of the
true children that had the Pentecostal baptism, and put
a heavy rebuke upon the counterfeit, in tongues, until
the counterfeits were silenced and condemned. God's
promises are true and sure.

People are trying to imitate the work of the Holy
Ghost these days, just as they did when the Lord sent
Moses to Pharaoh in Exodus 7 and 8, and gave him
a miracle or sign to show before Pharaoh, that when
Aaron should cast his rod before Pharaoh, it should
become a serpent. So when Pharaoh saw that Aaron's
rod had become a serpent, he called for his wise men and
the counterfeit sorcerers and magicians of Egypt. *"They
also did in like manner with their enchantments. For they
cast down every man his rod, and they became serpents: but
Aaron's rod swallowed up their rods"* (Exodus 7:11–12).
So the power of the Holy Ghost in God's people today
condemns and swallows up the counterfeit. It digs up
and exposes all the power of Satan—Christian Science,

theosophy, and spiritualism—all are uncovered before the Son of God. Glory to God!

Spiritualists have come to our meetings and had the demons cast out of them and have been saved and sanctified. Christian Scientists have come to the meetings and had the Christian Science demons cast out of them and have accepted the blood. *"Every plant, which my heavenly Father hath not planted, shall be rooted up"* (Matthew 15:13). People have come to this place full of demons and God has cast them out, and they have gone out crying with loud voices. Then when all the demons were cast out, they got saved, sanctified, and baptized with the Holy Ghost, clothed in their right minds and filled with glory and power. Dear loved ones, it is *"not by might, nor by power, but by my spirit, saith the* LORD*"* (Zechariah 4:6). *"Tarry ye in the city of Jerusalem, until ye be endued with power from on high"* (Luke 24:49); *"John truly baptized with water; but ye shall be baptized with the Holy Ghost not many days hence"* (Acts 1:5).

These were Jesus's departing words. May you tarry until you receive your personal Pentecost. Amen.

W. J. SEYMOUR
Vol. 1, No. 4

SIX

BEHOLD, THE BRIDEGROOM COMETH

"Then shall the kingdom of heaven be likened unto ten virgins, which took their lamps, and went forth to meet the bridegroom. And five of them were wise, and five were foolish. They that were foolish took their lamps, and took no oil with them: but the wise took oil in their vessels with their lamps. While the bridegroom tarried, they all slumbered and slept. And at midnight there was a cry made, Behold, the bridegroom cometh; go ye out to meet him. Then all those virgins arose, and trimmed their lamps. And the foolish said unto the wise, Give us of your oil; for our lamps are gone out ["going out" (RV)]. But the wise answered, saying, Not so; lest there be not enough for us and you: but go ye

rather to them that sell, and buy for yourselves. And while they went to buy, the bridegroom came; and they that were ready went in with him to the marriage: and the door was shut. Afterward came also the other virgins, saying, Lord, Lord, open to us. But he answered and said, Verily I say unto you, I know you not. Watch therefore, for ye know neither the day nor the hour wherein the Son of man cometh" (Matthew 25:1–13).

You know "virgin" in the Scripture is a type of purity. Christ is speaking in this parable about the church and its condition at His coming. Many precious souls today are not looking for the return of their Lord, and they will be found in the same condition as the five foolish virgins. They started out to meet the bridegroom, and had some oil in their lamps, but none in their vessels with their lamps. So when the cry was made to go forth, they were found wanting in oil, which is the real type of the Holy Ghost. Many of God's children are cleansed from sin and yet fight against getting more oil. They think they have enough.

They have some of God's love in their souls, but they have not the double portion of it. The thing they need is oil in their vessels with their lamps. It is just as plain as can be.

Dearly beloved, the Scripture says, *"Blessed are they which are called unto the marriage supper of the Lamb"* (Revelation 19:9). So they are blessed that have the call. Those that will be permitted to enter in are those who are justified, sanctified, and baptized with the Holy Ghost, sealed unto the day of redemption. Oh, may God stir up His waiting bride everywhere to get oil in their vessels with their lamps that they may enter into the marriage supper. The Holy Ghost is sifting out a people that are getting on the robes of righteousness and the seal in their foreheads. The angel is holding the winds now till all the children of God are sealed in their foreheads with the Father's name. Then the wrath of God is going to be poured out.

Behold, the Bridegroom cometh! Oh, the time is very near. All the testimonies of His coming that have been going on for months are a witness that He is coming soon. But when the trumpet sounds, it will be too late to prepare. Those that are not ready at the rapture will be left to go through the awful tribulation that is coming upon the earth. The wise virgins will be at the marriage supper and spend the time of the great tribulation with the Lord Jesus. They will have glorified bodies. For we which remain unto the coming of the Lord will be changed in the twinkling of an eye. (See 1 Corinthians 15:52.)

Many precious souls believe today that in sanctification, they have it all, that they have already the baptism with the Holy Ghost, or enduement of power; but in that day, they will find they are mistaken. They say, "Away with this third work." What is the difference, dear ones, if it takes 300 works? We want to be ready to meet the Bridegroom. The foolish virgins said to the wise, "Give us of your oil." This thing is going to happen. Many that are saying they have enough and are opposing will find their lamps going out and ask the prayers of God's people. God is warning you through His servants and handmaidens to get ready; but many are going to come back to get the oil from others. Dear ones, we cannot get more than enough for ourselves. You can grasp the saints' hands, but you cannot squeeze any oil out. You have to get the vessel filled for yourself. Many are going to be marrying and giving in marriage, buying and selling, and the cares of this world are going to get in the way. Above all, we want to get the oil, the Holy Ghost. Every Christian must be baptized with the Holy Ghost for himself. Many poor souls in that day will be awfully disappointed. May we seek Him today, the baptism with the Holy Ghost and fire. Now is the time to buy the oil; that is, by tarrying at the feet of the Lord Jesus and receiving the baptism with the Holy Spirit. It seems that people will be able to buy oil during the rapture. It seems that the Spirit will still be here on earth and that they could get it, but it will be too late for the marriage supper. So the Lord warns us to be ready, for we know not the day or the hour.

Those that are left in the rapture and still prove faithful to God and do not receive the mark of the beast, though they will have to suffer martyrdom, will be raised to reign with Christ. Antichrist will reign during the tribulation and everything will be controlled by him and by the false prophet, when they have succeeded in uniting the whole world in acknowledging the antichrist. Those that acknowledge him will be permitted to buy and sell, but those that stand faithful to the Lord Jesus and testify to the blood will be killed for the word of their testimony. (See Revelation 12:11.) But by proving faithful to death, they will be raised during the millennium and reign with Christ. But we that are caught up to the marriage supper of the Lamb will escape the plagues that are coming on the earth. May God fit every one of us for the coming of the Lord, that we may come back with Him on white horses and help Him to execute judgment on the earth and make way for the millennial kingdom when He shall reign from shore to shore, and righteousness shall cover the earth as waters cover the sea. (See Habakkuk 2:14.)

That is the time that Enoch prophesied of, *"Behold, the Lord cometh with ten thousand of his saints"* (Jude 1:14). *"Then shall the* LORD *go forth, and fight against those nations, as when he fought in the day of battle. And his feet shall stand in that day upon the mount of Olives"* (Zechariah 14:3–4). The mountain shall be parted in two. Then shall the antichrist and the false prophet be cast into the lake of fire and brimstone and Satan shall be bound a thousand years. (See Revelation 19:20; 20:2.)

We shall be priests and kings unto God, reigning with Him a thousand years in a jubilee of peace. Our

Christ will be King of Kings and Lord of Lords over the whole earth. We shall reign with Him over unglorified humanity. Some will be appointed over ten cities and some over two, and the twelve apostles will be over the twelve tribes of Israel. *"To him that overcometh will I grant to sit with me in my throne, even as I also overcame, and am set down with my Father in his throne"* (Revelation 3:21).

W. J. S.
Vol. 1, No. 5

SEVEN

RECEIVE YE THE HOLY SPIRIT

1. The first step in seeking the baptism of the Holy Spirit is to have a clear knowledge of the new birth in our souls that is the first work of grace and brings everlasting life to our souls. *"Therefore being justified by faith, we have peace with God"* (Romans 5:1). Every one of us that repents of our sins, and turns to the Lord Jesus with faith in Him, receives forgiveness of sins. Justification and regeneration are simultaneous. The pardoned sinner becomes a child of God in justification.

2. The next step for us is to have a clear knowledge, by the Holy Spirit, of the second work of grace wrought in our hearts by the power of the blood and the Holy

Spirit. Hebrews 10:14–15: *"For by one offering he hath perfected for ever them that are sanctified. Whereof the Holy Ghost also is a witness to us."* The Scripture also teaches, *"For both he that sanctifieth and they who are sanctified are all of one: for which cause he is not ashamed to call them brethren"* (Hebrews 2:11). We have Christ crowned and enthroned in our hearts, the tree of life. We have the brooks and streams of salvation flowing in our souls, but praise God, we can have the rivers. For the Lord Jesus says, "He that believeth on Me, as the Scripture hath said, out of his innermost being shall flow rivers of living water." This spoke He of the Spirit, for the Holy Spirit was not yet given. (See John 7:38–39.) However, praise our God, He is now given and being poured out upon all flesh. All races, nations, and tongues are receiving the baptism of the Holy Spirit and fire, according to the prophecy of Joel. (See Joel 2:28–30.)

3. When we have a clear knowledge of justification and sanctification, through the precious blood of Jesus Christ in our hearts, then we can be a recipient of the baptism of the Holy Spirit. Many people today are sanctified, cleansed from all sin, and perfectly consecrated to God, but they have never obeyed the Lord, according to Acts 1:4, 5, and 8, and Luke 24:39, for their real personal Pentecost, the enduement of power for service and work and for sealing unto the day of redemption. The baptism of the Holy Spirit is a gift without repentance, upon the sanctified, cleansed vessel. *"Now he which [established] us with you in Christ, and hath anointed us, is God; who*

hath also sealed us, and given the earnest of the Spirit in our hearts" (2 Corinthians 1:21–22). Praise our God for the sealing of the Holy Spirit unto the day of redemption.

Dearly beloved, the only people that will meet our Lord and Savior Jesus Christ, and go with Him into the marriage supper of the Lamb, are the wise virgins not only saved and sanctified, with pure and clean hearts, but having the baptism of the Holy Spirit. The others we find will not be prepared. They have some oil in their lamps but they have not the double portion of His Holy Spirit.

The disciples were filled with the unction of the Holy Spirit before Pentecost, which sustained them until they received the Holy Spirit baptism. Many people today are filled with joy and gladness, but they are far from the enduement of power. Sanctification brings rest, sweetness, and quietness to our souls. We are one with the Lord Jesus and are able to obey His precious Word, that *"man shall not live by bread alone, but by every word that proceedeth out of the mouth of God"* (Matthew 4:4), and we are feeding upon Christ.

However, let us wait for the promise of the Father upon our souls. According to Jesus's Word, *"John truly baptized with water; but ye shall be baptized with the Holy Ghost not many days hence....Ye shall receive power, after that the Holy Ghost is come upon you: and ye shall be witnesses unto me both in Jerusalem, and in all Judea, and in*

Samaria, and unto the uttermost part of the earth" (Acts 1:5, 8).

Glory! Glory! Hallelujah! Oh, worship, get down on your knees, and ask the Holy Spirit to come in, and you will find Him right at your heart's door, and He will come in. Prove Him now. Amen.

W. J. S.
Vol. 1, No. 5

EIGHT

GIFTS OF THE HOLY SPIRIT

"Now concerning spiritual gifts, brethren, I would not have you ignorant" (1 Corinthians 12:1).

Paul was speaking to the Corinthian church at this time. They were like Christ's people everywhere today. Many of His people do not know their privileges in this blessed gospel. The gospel of Christ *"is the power of God unto salvation to every one that believeth"* (Romans 1:16). And in order that we might know His power, we must forever abide in the Word of God that we may have the precious fruits of the Spirit, and not only the fruits but the precious gifts that Father has for His little ones.

Dearly beloved, may we search the Scriptures and see for ourselves whether we are measuring up to every word that proceedeth out of the mouth of God. If we will remain in the Scriptures and follow the blessed Holy Spirit all the way, we will be able to measure up to the Word of God in all of its fullness. Paul prayed in Ephesians 3:16–20, "*That he would grant you, according to the riches of his glory, to be strengthened with might by his Spirit in the inner man; that Christ may dwell in your hearts by faith; that ye, being rooted and grounded in love, may be able to comprehend with all saints what is the breadth, and length, and depth, and height; and to know the love of Christ, which passeth knowledge, that ye might be filled with all the fulness of God. Now unto him that is able to do exceeding abundantly above all that we ask or think, according to the power that worketh in us.*"

Many people say today that tongues are the least gift of any that the Lord can give, and they do not need it, and ask, "What good is it to us?"

By careful study of the Word, we see Paul telling the church to "*follow after charity, and desire spiritual gifts*" (1 Corinthians 14:1). Charity means divine love without which we will never be able to enter heaven. Gifts all will fall, but divine love will last through all eternity. And right in the same verse he says, "*Desire spiritual gifts, but rather that ye may prophesy,*" that is to say, preach in your own tongue that will build up the saints and the church.

But he says in the next verses, *"For he that speaketh in an unknown tongue speaketh not unto men, but unto God: for no man understandeth him; howbeit in the spirit he speaketh mysteries* ["hidden truth" (RV)]. *But he that prophesieth speaketh unto man to edification, and exhortation, and comfort"* (1 Corinthians 14:2–3). He that prophesies in his own tongue edifies the church; but he that speaks in unknown tongues edifies himself. His spirit is being edified, while the church is not edified, because they do not understand what he says unless the Lord gives somebody the interpretation of the tongue.

Here is where many stumble that have not this blessed gift to use in the Spirit. They say, "What good is it when you do not know what you are talking about?"

Praise God, every gift He gives is a good gift. It is very blessed, for when the Lord gets ready, He can speak in any language He chooses to speak. You ask, "Is not prophecy the best gift?" Prophecy is the best gift to the church, for it builds up the saints and edifies them and exalts them to higher things in the Lord Jesus. If a brother or sister is speaking in tongues and cannot speak any English, but preaches altogether in tongues, and has no interpretation, they are less than he that prophesies. But if they interpret, they are just as great.

May God help all of His precious people to read 1 Corinthians 14, and give them the real interpretation of the Word. May we all use our gift to the glory of God and not worship the gift. The Lord gives us power to use it to His own glory and honor. Many times, when we were receiving this blessed Pentecost, we all used to break out in tongues; but we have learned to be quieter with the gift. Often when God sends a blessed wave upon us, we all may speak in tongues for a while, but we will not keep it up while preaching service is going on, for we want to be obedient to the Word, that everything may *"be done decently and in order"* (1 Corinthians 14:40) and without confusion. Amen.

W. J. S.
Vol. 1, No. 5

NINE

REBEKAH: A TYPE OF THE BRIDE OF CHRIST

GENESIS 24

"*I pray thee: is there room in thy father's house for us to lodge in?*" (Genesis 24:23). These words were spoken by Eliezer, Abraham's eldest servant and steward of his house, to Rebekah when he had found her at the well in answer to his prayer. Eliezer, meaning "God's helper," is a type of the Holy Spirit, and Isaac is a type of Christ. Now as Eliezer was seeking a bride for Isaac, the son of Abraham, so the Holy Spirit today is seeking a bride for the Lord Jesus, God's only begotten Son.

Eliezer was sent to Abraham's country and to his kindred to take a wife for Isaac. So God our Father has sent the Holy Spirit from the glory land down into this world, and He, the Spirit of truth, is convicting the world of sin, righteousness, and judgment, and is selecting out of the body of Christ His bride. He is seeking among His kindred, the sanctified, and Jesus is baptizing them with the Holy Ghost and fire, preparing them for the great marriage supper of the Lamb. Praise our God! Eliezer was under oath not to select the bride from the Canaanites but from Abraham's kindred. So God is not selecting a bride for Christ among the sinners, for a sinner must first get saved and sanctified before he can be one with the Lord Jesus. Hebrews 2:11 says, *"For both he that sanctifieth and they who are sanctified are all of one: for which cause he is not ashamed to call them brethren."* So He is seeking a bride among His brethren, the sanctified.

"Christ also loved the church, and gave himself for it; that he might sanctify and cleanse it with the washing of water by the word, that he might present it to himself a glorious church, not having spot, or wrinkle, or any such thing; but that it should be holy and without blemish" (Ephesians 5:25–27). So Jesus today is selecting a sanctified people, baptizing them with the Holy Ghost and fire to greet Him at His coming. Rebekah was a virgin, the type of a sanctified soul. So the Holy Ghost today is standing at the heart of every pure virgin (sanctified soul) pleading, "I pray thee, is there room in thy heart that I may

come in and lodge?" Oh, beloved, we see many of the sanctified people today rejecting the Holy Spirit, just as people rejected Christ when He was on earth here.

It seems there is no room in their hearts for the baptism with the Holy Ghost and fire. May God help them to open their eyes and see that the time draws nigh for His coming. Oh, may Christ's waiting bride wake up and let the Holy Ghost come in.

Rebekah was a type of the wise virgins. When Eliezer met her at the well and asked her to let him drink a little water from her pitcher, oh how sweet and ready she was. She answered and said, *"Drink, my lord; and she hasted, and let down her pitcher upon her hand, and gave him drink"* (Genesis 24:18). And it pleased him. The Spirit is a Person. He can be pleased, He can be quenched, and He can be insulted, as we find Ananias insulted Him. (See Acts 5:3.) We please Him when we accept the words of Jesus. Then Jesus sends the Holy Spirit to witness in our hearts.

When Rebekah was done giving Eliezer a drink, she said, *"I will draw water for thy camels also"* (Genesis 24:19). Christ's bride must do everything without murmuring. Oh, how sweet it is when we have the mighty Spirit in our hearts; we are ready for service; we are ready for watering the whole entire world with the precious well of salvation in our heart. Beloved, when the Holy Ghost comes, He brings the well of salvation and rivers of living water.

"*And it came to pass, as the camels had done drinking, that the man took a gold earring of half a shekel weight, and two bracelets for her hands of ten shekels weight of gold*" (verse 22). Praise God. This is what our beloved sanctified people receive when they receive the witness of the anointing of the Holy Ghost upon their hearts, as when Jesus breathed upon the disciples before Pentecost in the upper room, where He said, "*Receive ye the Holy Ghost*" (John 20:22). The disciples had the witness in their hearts that very moment that "*both he that sanctifieth and they who are sanctified are all of one*" (Hebrews 2:11). For He had opened the Scriptures to them (see Luke 24:32), and their understanding was opened (see Luke 24:45). "*And their eyes were opened, and they knew him*" (Luke 24:31). So with us, when we receive sanctification and the witness of the Spirit in our hearts to our sanctification, the Scriptures are opened to us, we understand them, and our eyes are anointed. We see a picture of it in Rebekah.

When she had received Eliezer and let him drink out of her pitcher and had watered the camels, he gave her the earring and bracelets of gold. Oh, beloved, may we let the Holy Ghost sup out of our heart pitcher, for the Lord says, "*Behold, I stand at the door, and knock: if any man hear my voice, and open the door, I will come in to him, and will sup with him, and he with me*" (Revelation 3:20). And when He comes in, He opens His precious treasures to us, bracelets and earrings, great weights of gold. Oh, how blessed it is when the precious Spirit enters into our hearts like Eliezer. He tells us the great wealth of our Father and of our Christ, for He opens up our understanding, and enlightens our minds. His continual conversation is about the Father and Jesus. Eliezer was the very type of the Holy Spirit who takes the things of Christ and shows them unto us, for He told Rebekah of the wealth of Abraham and Isaac, giving her jewels. And she wore them, showing that she was the espoused of Isaac. (See Genesis 24.) Hallelujah! Jesus breathed the Holy Ghost on His disciples and said, *"Whose soever sins ye remit, they are remitted unto them; and whose soever sins yet retain, they are retained"* (John 20:23). Thus they had the witness in their hearts that they were candidates for the baptism with the Holy Ghost and fire.

He commanded them, *"Tarry ye in the city of Jerusalem, until ye be endued with power from on high"* (Luke 24:49). Praise our God!

"I pray thee: is there room in thy father's house for us to lodge in?" (Genesis 24:23). Beloved, is there room in your heart that God's blessed Spirit can come and lodge in? Rebekah was a wise virgin. She met Eliezer at the well and received the bracelets and earring, but she did not receive them until she had allowed him to drink out of her pitcher and had watered the camels. Many others stood by, no doubt, but they did not do any watering of the camels. Oh may all of Christ's waiting bride be filled

with the rivers of living water that they may water the thirsty, parched hearts with the rivers of salvation.

Rebekah wore her jewels. She did not put them aside or into her pocket, for we read that Laban saw them on his sister's hands. (See Genesis 24:30.) When we have received the abiding anointing in our hearts, someone can always see it shining forth upon our faces. Praise God!

When Eliezer had fed the camels and had come into the house, and when meat was set before him, he said, *"I will not eat, until I have told mine errand"* (verse 33). Oh beloved, we should be so zealous about the bride of Christ that nothing will be able to turn us aside. We find the first overthrow in the human soul was through the appetite; and when the Holy Ghost sends us on His mission, may we not be satisfied until we have told it, and of His coming back to earth again.

Then Eliezer told his mission: how Abraham had sent him to his kindred to take a wife for his son. Then he said, *"And now if ye will deal kindly and truly with my master, tell me: and if not, tell me"* (verse 49). They said, *"The thing proceedeth from the LORD"* (verse 50) and gave Rebekah to be the wife of his master's son. (See Genesis 24:51.) When people are living under the guidance of God's Holy Spirit, it does not take them very long to hear the voice of God, and they are willing to obey. Praise God! Then Eliezer ate and tarried with them that night, because he had received the desire of his master's heart and his own heart.

On the morrow, her brother and mother said, *"Let the damsel abide with us a few days, at the least ten,"* but Eliezer said, *"Hinder me not"* (verses 55–56). It is best, when we hear the words of God and the Spirit is upon us, to receive now the baptism with the Holy Spirit, instead of waiting two or three days and meeting friends and meeting the devil, who will try to persuade us out of it. If Rebekah had remained, perhaps her friends might have talked her out of going away with Eliezer over the plains, off to that distant land to her husband Isaac.

Eliezer said, *"Hinder me not."* Oh may we do nothing to hinder the entrance of the baptism with the Holy Ghost. We should see that everything is out of the way and nothing to stand between us and this glorious blessing. Then they called Rebekah and said to her, *"Wilt thou go with this man? And she said, I will go"* (verse 58). To receive the baptism with the Holy Ghost, we must forsake all and follow Jesus all the way. For the Lord Jesus says, *"For this cause shall a man leave his father and mother, and cleave to his wife"* (Mark 10:7). So we that are Christ's bride must forsake all and cleave to Christ, as Rebekah left father, mother, and brother, and rode on the camel to meet Isaac.

"And Isaac went out to meditate in the field at eventide: and he lifted up his eyes, and saw, and, behold, the camels were coming. And Rebekah lifted up her eyes, and when she

saw Isaac, she lighted off the camel" (Genesis 24:63–64). Now we are living in the eventide of this dispensation, when the Holy Spirit is leading us, Christ's bride, to meet Him in the clouds.

W. J. S.
Vol. 1, No. 6

TEN

THE BAPTISM WITH THE HOLY SPIRIT

Dear ones in Christ who are seeking the baptism with the Holy Ghost: do not seek for tongues but for the promise of the Father, and pray for the baptism with the Holy Ghost, and God will throw in the tongues according to Acts 2:4. We read in Acts 1:4–5, "*And, being assembled together with them, commanded them that they should not depart from Jerusalem, but wait for the promise of the Father, which, saith he, ye have heard of me. For John truly baptized with water; but ye shall be baptized with the Holy Ghost not many days hence.*"

This promise of the Father was preached unto the disciples by John the Baptist. And Jesus reminded the disciples about this baptism that John had preached to them in life. In England, we find the same thing. In Matthew 3:11, John, after warning the Jews and Pharisees against sin and hypocrisy, preached the doctrine of the baptism with the Holy Ghost. He said first in Matthew 3:8, *"Bring forth therefore fruits meet for repentance."* God is sending His precious ministers to preach repentance to the people, turn them from their sins, and cause them to make restitution according to their ability, and to have faith in the Lord Jesus Christ and be saved. Glory to God!

And then they must get sanctified through the precious blood of Jesus Christ, for He says in John 17:15–19, *"I pray not that thou shouldest take them out of the world, but that thou shouldest keep them from the evil. They are not of the world, even as I am not of the world. Sanctify them through thy truth: thy word is truth. As thou hast sent me into the world, even so have I also sent them into the world. And for their sakes I sanctify myself, that they also might be sanctified through the truth."* God wants His people to be sanctified, because He says again in Hebrews 13:12–13, *"Wherefore Jesus also, that he might sanctify the people with his own blood, suffered without the gate. Let us go forth therefore unto him without the camp, bearing his reproach."*

Then Jesus taught the disciples to tarry at Jerusalem. They obeyed Him and waited for the promise of the Father. *"And when the day of Pentecost was fully come, they were all with one accord in one place. And suddenly there came a sound from heaven as of a rushing mighty wind, and it filled all the house where they were sitting. And there appeared unto them cloven tongues like as of fire, and it sat upon each of them. And they were all filled with the Holy Ghost, and began to speak with other tongues, as the Spirit gave them utterance"* (Acts 2:1–4).

Wind is always typical of the Spirit or of life. *"And it filled all the house where they were sitting."* The rivers of salvation had come and had filled the whole place, and they all were immersed or baptized in the Holy Spirit. Praise God! *"And there appeared unto them cloven tongues like as of fire."* Beloved, when we receive the baptism with the Holy Ghost and fire, we surely will speak in tongues as the Spirit gives utterance. We are not seeking for tongues, but we are seeking the baptism with the Holy Ghost and fire. And when we receive it, we shall be so filled with the Holy Ghost that He Himself will speak in the power of the Spirit.

"And they were all filled with the Holy Ghost, and began to speak with other tongues, as the Spirit gave them utterance." Now, beloved, do not be too concerned about your speaking in tongues, but let the Holy Ghost give you utterance, and it will come just as freely as the air we breathe. It is nothing worked up, but it comes from the heart. *"With the heart man believeth unto righteousness; and with the mouth confession is made unto salvation"* (Romans 10:10). So when the Holy Ghost life comes in,

the mouth opens, through the power of the Spirit in the heart. Glory to God!

"There were dwelling at Jerusalem Jews, devout men, out of every nation under heaven. Now when this was noised abroad, the multitude came together, and were confounded, because that every man heard them speak in his own language. And they were all amazed and marvelled, saying one to another, Behold, are not all these which speak Galilaeans? And how hear we every man in our own tongue, wherein we were born?" (Acts 2:5–8).

Beloved, if you do not know the language that you speak, do not puzzle yourself about it, for the Lord did not promise us He would tell us what language we were speaking, but He promised us the interpretation of what we speak. In seeking the baptism, first get a clear, definite witness in your soul that you have the abiding Christ within. Then there will be no trouble in receiving the Pentecostal baptism, through faith in our Lord and Savior, Jesus Christ, for it is a free gift that comes without repentance. Bless His holy name!

W. J. S.
Vol. 1, No. 6

ELEVEN

THE HOLY SPIRIT, BISHOP OF THE CHURCH

It is the office work of the Holy Spirit to preside over the entire work of God on earth. (See Psalm 104:30.) Jesus was our Bishop while on earth, but now He has sent the Holy Ghost, amen, to take His place, not men. (See John 14:16; 15:26; 16:7–14). Praise His holy name!

The Holy Ghost is to infuse with divine power, and to invest with heavenly authority. No religious assembly is legal without His presence and His transaction.

We should recognize Him as the Teacher of teachers. The reason why there are so many of God's people without divine power today without experimental salvation, wrought out in their hearts by the blood, by the power of the blessed Holy Spirit, is because they have not accepted Him as their Teacher, as their Leader, as their Comforter. Jesus said in His precious Word that if He went away, He would send us another Comforter. The need of men and women today in their lives is a Comforter. Praise our God!

What matter where on earth we dwell

On Mountain top, or in the dell,

In cottage or a mansion fair,

Where Jesus is, 'tis heaven there.

Bless His holy name! May God help every one of His blood-bought children to receive this blessed Comforter. Glory to His name! Hallelujah! Hosanna to His omnipotent name! Oh, He is reigning in my soul! Hallelujah! I just feel like the song which says:

Oh, spread the tidings round

Whoever man is found,

Wherever human hearts

And human woes abound,

Let every Christian tongue

Proclaim the joyful sound,

The Comforter has come!

Many people today think we need new churches—that is to say church buildings, stone structures, brick structures, modern improvements, new choirs, trained singers right from the conservatories, paying from seven hundred to fifteen hundred dollars a year for singing, fine pews, fine chandeliers—everything that could attract the human heart to win souls to the meeting house is used in this twentieth century. We find that they have reached the climax, but all of that had failed to bring divine power and salvation to precious souls. Sinners have gone to the meeting house, heard a nice, fine, eloquent oration on Jesus, or on some particular church, or on some noted man. The people have been made glad to go because they have seen great wealth, they have seen people in the very latest styles, in different costumes, and loaded down with jewelry, decorated from head to foot with diamonds, gold, and silver.

The music in the church has been sweet, and it is found that a good many of the church people seem to be full of love, but there has always been a lack of power. We wonder why sinners are not being converted, and why it is that the church is always making improvements, and failing to do the work that Christ called her to do. It is because men have taken the place of Christ and the Holy Spirit. The church had the right idea that we need bishops and elders, but they must be given authority by our Lord and Savior Jesus Christ, and their qualifications for these offices must be the enduement of the power of the Holy Ghost.

Jesus, after choosing His disciples, said in John 15:16, "*Ye have not chosen me, but I have chosen you, and ordained you, that ye should go and bring forth fruit, and that your fruit should remain: that whatsoever ye shall ask of the Father in my name, he may give it to you.*" Praise our God! The Lord Jesus ordained His disciples with His own blessed hands before going back to glory, but He put the credentials in their hearts on the day of Pentecost, when they were baptized with the Holy Ghost and fire. Hallelujah! This was the authority that made them His witnesses unto the uttermost parts of the earth, for without the blessed Holy Spirit, in all of His fullness, we are not able to witness unto the uttermost parts of the earth. We must be coworkers with Him, partakers of the Holy Ghost. Then, when He is in us, in all of His fullness, He will manifest Himself. Signs and miracles will follow. This is the office work of the Holy Spirit in the churches. Amen.

I pray God that all Christ's people and ministers everywhere will please stop by the headquarters, the Jerusalem before God, for their credentials. Then they are entitled to receive credentials from the visible church. But the main credential is to be baptized with the Holy Ghost. Instead of new preachers from the theological schools and academies, the same old preachers, baptized with the Holy Ghost and fire, the same old deacons, and the same old plain church buildings will do. When the Holy Ghost comes in, He will cleanse out dead forms and ceremonies, and will give life and power to His ministers and preachers, in the same old church buildings. But without the Holy Ghost, they are simply tombstones. We must always recognize that a meeting house is simply a place where Christ's people gather to worship, and not the church. The church is planted in our hearts, through the blood of Jesus Christ, for Christ said in Matthew 16:18, *"Upon this rock I will build my church; and the gates of hell shall not prevail against it."* We see, if these meeting houses and such buildings were really churches of Christ, the storms, cyclones, and fire could not harm them; but we see them blown down by storms and burned down. But through the precious blood of Christ, this church that He plants in our souls will stand throughout eternity.

The first thing in every assembly is to see that He, the Holy Ghost, is installed as the chairman. The reason why we have so many dried-up missions and churches today is because they have not the Holy Ghost as the chairman. They have some man in His place. Man is all right in his place—that is when he is filled with the power of the Holy Ghost, for it is not man that does the work, but the Holy Ghost from the glory land, sent by Jesus to work through this tabernacle of clay. Wherever you find the Holy Ghost as the chairman in any assembly, you will find a fruitful assembly, you will find children being born unto God.

Just as it takes a father and a mother to bring forth children of this natural life, so it takes the Word and the Spirit to bring forth children of the spiritual birth. There must be a father and there must be a mother. God chooses human instruments to preach the Word unto the people, and the Holy Ghost gives birth to everyone who receives the Word of Christ, which means the new birth. Praise our God. Where a Holy Ghost man preaches the Word of God, the Lord will bring forth sons and daughters unto his administration.

Jesus Christ is the archbishop of these assemblies, and He must be recognized. Also we must recognize the Holy Spirit in all of His office work. He takes the members into the church, which is the body of Christ. Through repentance to God, and faith in Jesus, they become the members of the church of Christ. And they remain members as long as they live free from sin. When they commence sinning, the Holy Ghost, the chairman and bishop, the presiding elder, turns them out, and they know when they are turned out of this church. They don't have to go and ask their pastor or their preacher, for they feel within their own soul that the glory has left them—the joy, the peace, the rest and comfort. Then when they feel the lack in their souls, if they will confess their sins, God, the Holy Ghost, will accept them back into the church.

Oh, thank God for this holy way. I am so glad that sham battles are over. Men and women must live straight, holy, pure lives, free from sin, or else they have no part with Christ Jesus. When men and women are filled with the Holy Ghost, everywhere they go, living waters will flow. The Lord promised that out of our innermost being living rivers of water should flow. (See John 7:38.) This is the Holy Ghost. Amen!

The mighty Pison, the Gihon, the Hiddekel, and the Euphrates of our soul will flow, representing the rivers of salvation. Amen!

W. J. S.
Vol. 1, No. 9

TWELVE

LETTER TO ONE SEEKING THE HOLY GHOST

Dear Beloved in Christ Jesus,

The Lord Jesus has said in His precious Word, *"Blessed are they which do hunger and thirst after righteousness: for they shall be filled"* (Matthew 5:6). God's promises are true and sure. We can rest upon His promises. He says, *"Blessed are the pure in heart: for they shall see God"* (Matthew 5:8). *"Blessed are the poor in spirit: for theirs is the kingdom of heaven"* (Matthew 5:3).

The Lord Jesus is always ready to fill the hungry, thirsty soul, for He said in His precious Word, *"He that believeth on me, as the scripture hath said, out of his belly* shall flow rivers of living water. (*But this spake he of the Spirit, which they that believe on him should receive: for the Holy Ghost was not yet given; because that Jesus was not yet glorified)*" (John 7:38–39). But, praise God, He is given to us today.

All we have to do it to obey the first chapter of Acts, and wait for the promise of the Father upon our souls. The Lord Jesus said in His precious Word, "*Behold, I send the promise of my Father upon you: but tarry ye in the city of Jerusalem, until ye be endued with power from on high*" (Luke 24:49).

"*For John truly baptized with water; but ye shall be baptized with the Holy Ghost not many days hence…. Ye shall receive power, after that the Holy Ghost is come upon you: and ye shall be witnesses unto me both in Jerusalem, and in all Judea, and in Samaria, and unto the uttermost part of the earth*" (Acts 1:5, 8). They tarried until they received the mighty power of the baptism with the Holy Spirit upon their souls. Then God put the credentials in their hearts, and put the ring of authority on their finger, and sealed them in the forehead with the Father's name, and wrote on their heart the name of the New Jerusalem, and put in their hand the stone with the name written that no man knoweth save he that receiveth it. (See Revelation 2:17.) Praise the Lord, for His mercy endureth forever. Let us stand upon His promises. They are sure, they will not break.

The Lord Jesus says, *"Behold, I give unto you power to tread on serpents and scorpions, and over all the power of the enemy: and nothing shall by any means hurt you"* (Luke 10:19). Dear loved one, the Lord Jesus when He rose from the dead, said, *"All power is given unto me in heaven and in earth. Go ye therefore, and teach all nations, baptizing them in the name of the Father, and of the Son, and of the Holy Ghost"* (Matthew 28:18–19). *"He that believeth and is baptized shall be saved; but he that believeth not shall be damned. And these signs shall follow them that believe; in my name shall they cast out devils; they shall speak with new tongues; they shall take up serpents; and if they drink any deadly thing, it shall not hurt them; they shall lay hands on the sick, and they shall recover.... And they went forth, and preached every where, the Lord working with them, and confirming the word with signs following"* (Mark 16:16–18, 20). Praise His dear name, for He is just the same today.

The first thing in order to receive this precious and wonderful baptism with the Holy Spirit, we want to have a clear knowledge of justification by faith according to the Bible. Romans 5:1 says, *"Therefore being justified by faith, we have peace with God through our Lord Jesus Christ"*—faith that all our actual sins may be washed away. Actual sin means committed sin.

And then the second step is to have a real knowledge of sanctification, which frees us from original sin—the sin that we were born with, which we inherited from our father Adam. We were not responsible for that sin until we received light, for we could not repent of a sin that we did not commit. When we came to the Lord as a sinner, we repented to God of our actual sins, and God for Christ's sake pardoned us and washed our sin and pollution away, and planted eternal life in our souls.

Afterwards we saw in the Word of God, *"This is the will of God, even your sanctification"* (1 Thessalonians 4:3). (See also John 17:15–19.) We consecrated ourselves to God, and the Lord Jesus sanctified our souls, and made us every whit clean. Then after we were clearly sanctified, we prayed to God for the baptism with the Holy Spirit. So He sent the Holy Spirit to our hearts and filled us with His blessed Spirit, and He gave us the Bible evidence, according to Acts 2:1–4, speaking with other tongues as the Spirit gives utterance.

Praise our God, He is the same yesterday, today, and forever. (See Hebrews 13:8.) Receive Him just now and He will fill you. Amen. Don't get discouraged but pray until you are filled, for the Lord says, *"Men ought always to pray, and not to faint"* (Luke 18:1). Don't stop because you do not receive the baptism with the Holy Ghost at the first, but continue until you are filled. The Lord Jesus told His disciples to tarry until they were endued with power from on high. Many people today are willing to tarry just so long, and then they give up and fail to receive their personal Pentecost that would measure with the Bible. The Lord Jesus says, *"Ye shall be filled*" (Luke 6:21). He says that to the person that hungers and thirsts after righteousness and He says they are blessed. So if there is a hunger and thirst in our souls for righteousness, we are blessed of Him. Praise His dear name!

YOURS IN CHRIST,
W. J. S.
Vol. 1, No. 9

THIRTEEN

TESTIMONY AND PRAISE TO GOD

Oh, I feel the coming of our Lord and Savior Jesus Christ drawing nigh. Hallelujah! Glory to His name! I am so glad that the Lord is holding the winds until the angel has sealed all of the saints of the living God in their foreheads, the baptism of the Holy Spirit. The midnight cry will soon be made, when the morning and the night shall come. It will be morning in our souls, to those that are waiting for His coming! The awful black night of tribulation as the black night of Egypt will come upon all the world. May God help all of His precious waiting bride to be watching, waiting until our Lord shall come.

Oh, I am so thankful that I can work for my Christ and my God. The time is short when our blessed Jesus shall return to this earth, and snatch away His waiting bride. After six thousand years of toil and labor, we are going to have one thousand years of rest with our Lord and Savior, Jesus Christ. Glory to His holy name!

I can't forget how, kneeling at the dear old board in Azusa Street, I promised God I would go where He wanted me to go and stay where He wanted me to stay, and be what He wanted me to be. I meant every word of it and God has taken me at my word. How His glory is flooding my soul. Oh, how I worship His precious name! I have to stop and wonder how God can bless the Word through me. To think He has saved me when all my family were infidels and everything that would drive me from God. No one can ever know how I feel for the way God has dealt with me. Oh, how I love Jesus. It thrills my very being to think of the blood. It has done so much for me. I am filled with wonder love, and praise that God would permit me to see the workings of His mighty power in these last days. Oh, to think we have lived to see the return of the apostolic power and to see the gifts restored back to the church. I find we cannot compromise with anything or anybody. Oh, we must stand for all the light we have received, *"and having done all, to stand"* (Ephesians 6:13).

BROTHER SEYMOUR
312 AZUSA ST.
LOS ANGELES
Vol. 1, No. 9

FOURTEEN

THE ORDINANCES TAUGHT BY OUR LORD

We believe in three ordinances in the church: foot washing, the Lord's Supper, and water baptism.

FOOT WASHING (JOHN 13)

Dear loved ones, it is so sweet to think of that wonderful love that our Christ has for His dear people. Oh beloved, just think of our Almighty Christ becoming a servant, washing the disciples' feet. This is the first place in the Scriptures where we see Jesus using water, a very type of regeneration, washing the disciples' feet.

Regeneration is spoken of as *"the washing of water by the word"* (Ephesians 5:26). So this ordinance is a type of regeneration. Jesus is the Word. *"Now ye are clean through the word which I have spoken unto you"* (John 15:3).

Jesus washed the disciples' feet, and exhorted them to humility and charity. Bless His holy name. We read in the Word of God, *"Now before the feast of the passover, when Jesus knew that his hour was come that he should depart out of this world unto the Father, having loved his own which were in the world, he loved them unto the end"* (John 13:1). Bless God! Praise His holy name! *"And supper being ended, the devil having now put into the heart of Judas Iscariot, Simon's son, to betray him; Jesus knowing that the Father had given all things into his hands, and that he was come from God, and went to God; he riseth from supper, and laid aside his garments; and took a towel, and girded himself. After that he poureth water into a bason, and began to wash the disciples' feet, and to wipe them with the towel wherewith he was girded"* (John 13:2–5).

We read where Jesus *"cometh to Simon Peter: and Peter saith unto him, Lord, dost thou wash my feet? Jesus answered and said unto him, What I do thou knowest not now; but thou shalt know hereafter"* (John 13:6–7). We can see that this was something new to Peter. He was not used to the Master's washing his feet. But the Lord Jesus told him he should know hereafter. What Jesus means was that when the blessed Holy Spirit should be poured out after the resurrection and ascension unto heaven, that this blessed Holy Spirit would lead Peter into all the doctrines of Jesus, and they would be practiced just as Jesus said in John 16:12–14, *"I have yet many things to say unto you, but ye cannot bear them now. Howbeit when he, the Spirit of truth, is come, he will guide you into all truth: for he shall not speak of himself; but whatsoever he shall hear, that shall he speak: and He will shew you things to come. He shall glorify me: for he shall receive of mine, and shall shew it unto you."*

Peter said to Him, *"Thou shalt never wash my feet. Jesus answered him, If I wash thee not, thou hast no part with me"* (John 13:8). Dear beloved, none of us should reject the command of our Lord and Savior, Jesus Christ, or these different ordinances that He has instituted. What right have we to dictate to our blessed Master? He said so tenderly, *"If I wash thee not, thou hast no part with me."* And this was a rebuke also to any man or any woman that thinks they are independent of the teachings of Jesus. So when Peter heard this rebuke, he said to the Lord, *"Lord, not my feet only, but also my hands and my head"* (verse 9). How these disciples loved Jesus after that. Jesus said to him, *"He that is washed needeth not save to wash his feet, but is clean every whit: and ye are clean, but not all"* (verse 10).

"So after he had washed their feet, and had taken his garments, and was set down again, he said unto them, Know ye what I have done to you? Ye call me Master and

Lord: and ye say well; for so I am. If I then, your Lord and Master, have washed your feet; ye also ought to wash one another's feet" (John 13:12–14). Why? Well we only have to read the next verse for ourselves, *"For I have given you an example."* Dear beloved, we can see this is humility towards each other in real love. While it does mean that, suppose we all practice it literally, for Jesus is our example. He said, *"I have given you an example, that ye should do as I have done to you."* Some may say that the manner and customs have changed from that day, as we no longer wear sandals, but, dear ones, are our manners and customs going to change the Word of God? *"Verily, verily, I say unto you, The servant is not greater than his lord; neither he that is sent greater than he that sent him. If ye know these things, happy are ye if ye do them"* (John 13:16–17). Now this is to His true believers, because they are worthy. Verse 18 explains just who should not do it; He says, *"I speak not of you all: I know whom I have chosen."* Dear beloved, if the Lord has chosen us, He has chosen us to *"walk in the light, as he is in the light, we have fellowship one with another, and the blood of Jesus Christ his Son cleanseth us from all sin"* (1 John 1:7). Amen.

Jesus Himself instituted foot washing in the New Testament, not as in the Old Testament, when the priest would wash his own feet at the laver in the temple, which represented regeneration, but Jesus Himself washed the disciples' feet and wiped them with the towel. So, dear loved ones, we believe that foot washing is one of the ordinances of the church of God. We find that it is a service much blest of God to our souls. It is for the disciples, not for sinners. In this service, the sisters will assemble by themselves apart and wash each other's feet and the brothers will wash the brothers' feet. This is also a service of testimony, song, and praise. After that comes the Lord's Supper.

THE LORD'S SUPPER

The Lord Jesus ate the Passover with His disciples, which was the law of Moses. It was now finished forever, as He shoved that table aside, and after washing the disciples' feet, instituted the Lord's Supper, the Christian Passover, the bread and the wine.

The Passover was the very type of Jesus. It had a threefold meaning: the sprinkled blood for redemption; the body of the Lamb eaten for health and healing; and the passing over the Red Sea, which was a type of the blood of Jesus Christ that gives us victory over all the powers of the enemy. *"The Lord Jesus the same night in which he was betrayed took bread: and when he had given thanks, he brake it, and said, Take, eat: this is my body, which is broken for you: this do in remembrance of me. After the same manner also he took the cup, when he had supped, saying, this cup is the new testament in my blood: this do ye, as oft as ye drink it, in remembrance of me. For as often as ye eat this bread, and drink this cup, ye do shew the Lord's death till he come"* (1 Corinthians 11:23–26). Praise His holy name. So we see that this ordinance points us to the coming of the Lord, our great deliverance, as the Passover was the deliverance of the children of Israel from Egypt.

The Passover supper always reminded the Jews of God's great love for them in delivering them out of Egyptian bondage. But it was by blood which pointed them to the Lamb of Calvary. So the Lord's Supper is to us a memorial of the death of our Lord and also points us to His coming to catch us away in the glorious liberty of the children of God.

They ate the Passover, the body of the Lamb, which gave them strength and healing, so the body of the Lamb stood for healing and health, just as Christ's body is health to us, for with His stripes, you are healed. (See Isaiah 53:5.) We find as we partake of this ordinance, it brings healing to our bodies if we discern the Lord's body by faith. It also teaches us salvation and sanctification through the blood. Our souls are built up, for we eat His flesh and drink His blood. The Lord Jesus promised, *"Man shall not live by bread alone, but by every word that proceedeth out of the mouth of God"* (Matthew 4:4). May Christ's children everywhere live by every word that proceedeth out of the mouth of God.

WATER BAPTISM

We believe in water baptism, because Jesus commanded it after His resurrection.

"He that believeth and is baptized shall be saved" (Mark 16:16). We believe in water by immersion, single. "And Jesus, when he was baptized, went up straightway out of the water" (Matthew 3:16). "And he commanded the chariot to stand still: and they went down both into the water, both Philip and the eunuch; and he baptized him. And when they were come up out of the water, the Spirit of the Lord caught away Philip, that the eunuch saw him no more: and he went on his way rejoicing" (Acts 8:38–39).

It sets forth the believer with Christ in death, burial, and resurrection. "Know ye not, that so many of us as were baptized into Jesus Christ were baptized into his death? Therefore we are buried with him by baptism into death: that like as Christ was raised up from the dead by the glory of the Father, even so we also should walk in newness of life. For if we have been planted together in the likeness of his death, we shall be also in the likeness of his resurrection" (Romans 6:3–5). "For as many of you as have been baptized into Christ have put on Christ" (Galatians 3:27).

Baptism is not a saving ordinance, but it is essential because it is a command of our Lord. (See Mark 16:16.) "Repent, and be baptized every one of you in the name of Jesus Christ for the remission of sins" (Acts 2:38). It is "not the putting away of the filth of the flesh, but the answer of a good conscience toward God" (1 Peter 3:21). It is obedience to the command of Jesus, following saving faith. We believe every true believer will practice it. It should be administered by a disciple who is baptized with the

Holy Ghost and fire, in the name of the Father, Son, and Holy Ghost. *"Go ye therefore, and teach all nations, baptizing them in the name of the Father, and of the Son, and of the Holy Ghost: teaching them to observe all things whatsoever I have commanded you"* (Matthew 28:19–20). But we find that they were first to tarry for the promise of the Father which would qualify them. *"And being assembled together with them, commanded them that they should not depart from Jerusalem, but wait for the promise of the Father"* (Acts 1:4).

We believe that we should teach God's people to observe all things whatsoever He has commanded us, practicing every command and living by every word that proceedeth out of the mouth of God. This is a full gospel.

Bible salvation will take you into heaven, but if you have not got Bible salvation, you will have a great deal of trouble around the gate. Your name will not be found. We are not called by this country to preach the gospel, but we are called from heaven—and heaven is not bankrupt, neither has God gone out of business. He does not send us out to preach this gospel and not pay our bills. Do business for Christ and He will take care of you.

"God so loved the world, that he gave his only begotten Son, that whosoever believeth in him should not perish, but have everlasting life" (John 3:16). Oh today if you have the Lord Jesus Christ in your heart, you have everlasting life. This salvation is real; it is not an influence.

Out of His side flowed blood and water. The blood represents cleansing and the water the baptism with the Holy Ghost. The rivers of living water that Jesus promised flowed out of His side. We get all of this by living in Christ.

The Lord has provided the Word as a looking glass for us to see ourselves whether there are any spots on us. And the Word is a washer. *"Ye are clean through the word which I [Christ] have spoken unto you"* (John 15:3).

When you are sanctified, the old Ishmael of your soul is put out of your house. You are free from the old man. Old Ishmael will not pinch little Isaac any more to make him cry. Jesus Christ is enthroned in that house.

Oh it is so precious to have the Lord Jesus crowned in your heart. How wonderfully and sweetly the Spirit unfolds the Scriptures to you. You receive the Holy Ghost and He unravels everything from Genesis to Revelation. He starts and unfolds and all you do is to follow on.

The Jews were the very fig tree that the Lord planted. He planted it that the scepter might not depart from Judah. Herod was the first foreign king that swayed the scepter over God's people. And right at that time, Christ was born and the government was upon His shoulder. (See Isaiah 9:6.) This fulfilled Genesis 49:10.

Freeloveism and everything of that kind is from the pit of hell. It is a dragon to devour those who get out of the Word. But praise God, He has given to His children to know these spirits. Such spirits will not be allowed, any more than magicians, soothsayers, and sorcerers were allowed to be among God's children in the early days.

If you have carnality in your heart and do not get it out, you do not know where it will lead you. As soon as you get the light of sanctification, you must seek at once the cleansing blood or you will lose all your salvation.

We believe in a real salvation that gives you the witness by the Spirit. Calvin taught a salvation that if you said you had it, you did not have it; and if you had it, you did not know it; and if you lost it, you could not get it again.

Wesley taught that if you had it, you would know it, and if you lost it, you could get it again. Jesus taught, *"He that believeth on the Son of God hath the witness in himself"* (1 John 5:10). We teach that if a man is ensnared by the devil, and has not trampled the blood of Jesus Christ under his feet and counted the blood wherewith he was sanctified an unholy thing, he can get back to Jesus Christ by restitution and faith and doing his first works over.

If your heart is open to the blood of Christ, He will save you. All He wants is a repentant heart that has godly sorrow for sin, and He will wash you. Though your sins be red like crimson, they shall be as wool. (See Isaiah 1:18.) Oh the promises of God are sure and steadfast, and though the heaven and earth pass away, the promises of Jesus will never pass away. (See Matthew 24:35.) As long as there is breath and life in your body, you can look up to Jesus and He will save you, but if there is no repentance in your heart, you would have no desire to be saved. But, beloved, if there is one particle of desire in your heart to look to God, you have not sinned away your day of grace. They that have sinned away their day of grace cannot be stirred any more than a chair. No appeal will move them. Christ has a desire to save every man and woman on the face of the earth.

We do not read anything in the Word about writing in unknown languages, so we do not encourage that in our meetings. Let us measure everything by the Word, that all fanaticism may be kept out of the work. We have found it questionable whether any real good has come out of such writing.

A sister who was baptized in the stream at the campground says that when she came to change her clothing, she attempted to put on her jewelry again, but the Spirit would not let her, so she left it off. While one sister was under the power, her hands went up and took the fancy pins out of her hat and threw them away and she never put them on again. So the Spirit has been working in harmony with the Word, teaching His people how to dress according to the Bible. Gold watches, rings, etc., have disappeared, and gone into sending the gospel.

From missionaries in Macao, China, we received word that some of the Chinese Christians have received the baptism with the Holy Ghost and are speaking in new tongues.

W. J. Seymour
No. 1, Vol. 10

FIFTEEN

THE MARRIAGE TIE

Marriage is a divine institution which God Himself has instituted. *"And the LORD God said, It is not good that man should be alone; I will make him an help meet for him.... Therefore shall a man leave his father and his mother, and shall cleave unto his wife: and they shall be one flesh"* (Genesis 2:18, 24). *"Neither was the man created for the woman; but the woman for the man"* (1 Corinthians 11:9).

God commended it. *"Whoso findeth a wife findeth a good thing, and obtaineth favour of the LORD"* (Proverbs 18:22; see also Genesis 2:18).

God is in it. "*And he answered and said unto them, Have ye not read, that he which made them at the beginning made them male and female...? Wherefore they are no more twain, but one flesh. What therefore God hath joined together, let not man put asunder*" (Matthew 19:4–6).

It is honorable in all. "*Marriage is honourable in all, and the bed undefiled: but whoremongers and adulterers God will judge*" (Hebrews 13:4).

Christ attended a wedding in Cana. He went to adorn it, to beautify it with His presence. "*And the third day there was a marriage in Cana of Galilee; and the mother of Jesus was there: and both Jesus was called, and his disciples, to the marriage*" (John 2:1–2).

The forbidding to marry is the doctrine of devils. "*Now the Spirit speaketh expressly, that in the latter times some shall depart from the faith, giving heed to seducing spirits, and doctrines of devils...forbidding to marry*" (1 Timothy 4:1, 3).

MARRIAGE BINDING FOR LIFE

God has approved of but one wife and one husband. "*Therefore shall a man leave his father and his mother, and shall cleave unto his wife: and they shall be one flesh*" (Genesis 2:24). "*The Pharisees also came unto him, tempting him, and saying unto him, Is it lawful for a man to put away his wife for every cause? And he answered and said unto them, Have ye not read, that he which made them*

*at the beginning made them male and female, and said,
For this cause shall a man leave father and mother, and
shall cleave to his wife: and they twain shall be one flesh?
Wherefore they are no more twain, but one flesh. What
therefore God hath joined together, let not man put asunder"* (Matthew 19:3–6).

The husband and wife are bound together for life.
*"For the woman which hath an husband is bound by the
law to her husband so long as he liveth; but if the husband be
dead, she is loosed from the law of her husband"* (Romans
7:2). *"The wife is bound by the law as long as her husband
liveth; but if her husband be dead, she is at liberty to be married to whom she will; only in the Lord"* (1 Corinthians
7:39).

No court of man should sever the marriage tie.
*"Wherefore they are no more twain, but one flesh. What
therefore God hath joined together, let not man put asunder"* (Matthew 19:6). Death alone severs the marriage
tie.

MOSES'S LAW OF DIVORCE

Under Moses's law, God suffered men to divorce
their wives and marry again because of the hardness of
their hearts. *"They say unto him, Why did Moses then
command to give a writing of divorcement, and to put her
away? He saith unto them, Moses because of the hardness
of your hearts suffered you to put away your wives: but from*

the beginning it was not so" (Matthew 19:7–8). Under Moses's law, they had been accustomed, for any uncleanness, adultery, fornication, or some cause not as much as that, to put away the wife by giving her a bill of divorcement, and she could go and be another man's wife. But under the New Testament law, the law of Christ, she is bound by the law to her husband till death.

THE EDENIC STANDARD OF MATRIMONY

Jesus did away with the divorce law, and restored matrimony back to the Edenic standard. Under Moses's law, the sacredness of matrimony was lost through the hardness of hearts. But under the law of grace, it is restored back as in the beginning of grace. Praise God! God's promises are true and sure. Hallelujah! Amen.

Under the New Testament law, the law of Christ, there is but one cause for which a man may put away his wife, but no right to marry again. This cause is fornication or adultery. *"It hath been said, Whosoever shall put away his wife, let him give her a writing of divorcement: but I say unto you, That whosoever shall put away his wife, saving for the cause of fornication, causeth her to commit adultery: and whosoever shall marry her that is divorced committeth adultery"* (Matthew 5:31–32). *"And I say unto you, Whosoever shall put away his wife, except it be for fornication, and shall marry another, committeth adultery: and whoso marrieth her which is put away doth commit adultery"* (Matthew 19:9). These two Scriptures are just the same in meaning. Matthew 5:31–32 is the key to the whole subject. It settles the question.

FORBIDDEN TO MARRY AGAIN

After a man has lawfully put away his wife, or a wife has lawfully put away her husband, they are positively forbidden to marry again, under the New Testament law, until the former companion is dead. *"And he saith unto them, Whosoever shall put away his wife, and marry another, committeth adultery against her. And if a woman shall put away her husband, and be married to another, she committeth adultery"* (Mark 10:11–12). *"Whosoever putteth away his wife, and marrieth another, committeth adultery: and whosoever marrieth her that is put away from her husband committeth adultery"* (Luke 16:18). *"For the woman which hath an husband is bound by the law to her husband so long as he liveth; but if the husband be dead, she is loosed from the law of her husband. So then if, while her husband liveth, she be married to another man, she shall be called an adulteress: but if her husband be dead, she is free from that law; so that she is no adulteress, though she be married to another man"* (Romans 7:2–3).

ADULTERY AND FORNICATION

The act of adultery is between a married person and another who is not the lawful companion. Both parties may be married or only one. When only one is married, the act is called fornication. Jesus said, *"Whosoever* shall put away his wife, saving for the cause of fornication, causeth her to commit adultery" (Matthew 5:32; see also Matthew 19:9). These sins are just the same, only one is committed while living with a husband and the other is when one has separated and married again.

No man can enter the kingdom of heaven without confessing and forsaking adultery and fornication. "*Now the works of the flesh are manifest, which are these; adultery, fornication, uncleanness, lasciviousness…envyings, murders, drunkenness, revellings, and such like: of the which I tell you before, as I have also told you in time past, that they which do such things shall not inherit the kingdom of God*" (Galatians 5:19, 21). "*Let the wicked forsake his way, and the unrighteous man his thoughts: and let him return unto the* LORD, *and he will have mercy upon him; and to our God, for he will abundantly pardon*" (Isaiah 55:7).

THE INNOCENT PARTY

If Jesus had intended that the innocent party should marry, He would have said so, and would not have said, "Moses suffered it because of the hardness of your hearts." Jesus makes it very plain. If the innocent party marries, they are living in adultery. Jesus is showing the sacredness of matrimony. Dear beloved, let us obey God in spite of everything. There is one Scripture where many people are tied up, and it is Matthew 19:9, where Jesus said, "*I say unto you, Whosoever shall put away his wife, except it to be for fornication, and shall marry another, committeth adultery: and whoso marrieth her which is put away doth commit adultery.*" Now dear loved ones, let us stop and pray over this. "Except it be for fornication and marrieth another." Some think that this party would be entitled to marry again, but let us stop and see what Jesus is teaching here. If he puts away his wife except for the cause of fornication, he commits a sin, because he will cause her to commit adultery. Therefore he is bound by the law as long as she lives, bound right to the Edenic standard. Amen.

Dear loved ones, if Jesus had instituted that the innocent party could get another wife, He would be instituting the same thing that was permitted by Moses, and would have the church filled with that today.

Now the reason Jesus gave him permission to put away his wife for the cause of fornication was that she is already adulterous, so her adultery gave him a lawful right to separate. While it gives him that right, yet it does not give him the right to get another wife while she lives.

Paul in 1 Timothy 3:2 says, "*A bishop then must be blameless, the husband of one wife.*" He also says, in 1 Timothy 5:9, "*Let not a widow be taken into the number under threescore years old, having been the wife of one man.*" This shows plainly that they recognized in the church that a man was to have one wife and a woman one husband.

AFTER LIGHT HAS COME

Romans 7:2–3 and 1 Corinthians 7:39 give us very clear light. Oh may God help us to accept Bible salvation, instead of having our opinion and losing our souls. Dear beloved, you that have two wives or two husbands, before you had light on it, you lived that way and had no condemnation. God did not condemn you until you received the light upon His Word on this subject; but now God holds you responsible for the light. If you continue in the old life after light has come upon you, then you will be in the sight of God an adulterer or an adulteress, and you are bound to lose your experience or substitute something in the place of what God hath wrought. *"If we walk in the light, as he is in the light, we have fellowship one with another, and the blood of Jesus Christ his Son cleanseth us from all sin"* (1 John 1:7). Let us obey God's Word if it takes our right eye or right hand. (See Matthew 5:29–30.)

So we find under the New Testament there is no putting away the first wife and getting another. Death is the only thing that severs the marriage tie. (See Romans 7:2; 1 Corinthians 7:39.)

W. J. SEYMOUR
Vol. 1, No. 10

SIXTEEN

CHRIST'S MESSAGES TO THE CHURCH

The last message given to the church was by the Holy Ghost, from our Lord and Savior Jesus Christ through Brother John on the Isle of Patmos. Dear beloved, we read these words in Revelation 1:5–7, *"Unto him that loved us, and washed us from our sins in his own blood"*—hallelujah to His name!—*"and hath made us kings and priests unto God and his Father; to him be glory and dominion for ever and ever. Amen. Behold, he cometh with clouds; and every eye shall see him, and they also which pierced him; and all kindreds of the earth shall wail because of him. Even so, Amen."*

This is the beginning of this wonderful and blessed message given to our beloved apostle John while he was suffering for the Word of God and for the testimony of Jesus Christ. Jesus knew all about His servant, though He had been living in heaven more than half a century after His ascension. And He came and visited that beloved apostle, the disciple who loved Jesus and leaned on His bosom. John was now old but had been faithful to the trust that Jesus had given him. He had passed through awful trials and tribulations for this precious gospel, even being boiled in a cauldron of oil, tradition tells us; but, blessed be God, they were not able to kill him. And when they got tired of this precious Holy Ghost gospel messenger, preaching to them the faith of Jesus, they banished him to the Isle of Patmos. And while he was in the Spirit on the Lord's Day, our blessed Jesus Christ, the Son of the living God, our great Redeemer, came and gave him this wonderful revelation, and introduced Himself to John. "*I am Alpha and Omega, the beginning and the ending, saith the Lord, which is, and which was, and which is to come, the Almighty*" (verse 8). Hallelujah.

Oh beloved, the Lord Jesus knows all about our trials and tribulations, because He was a man of sorrows and acquainted with grief. (See Isaiah 53:3.) His whole life was a life of suffering. We read in Hebrews 5:8–9, "*Though he were a Son, yet learned he obedience by the things which he suffered; and being made perfect, he became the author of eternal salvation unto all them that obey him.*"

Oh bless our God. Just to think that Jesus was God's Son, and all things were made by Him and for Him, yet He was foreordained before the foundation of the world that He should die. He was slain before the foundation of the world. So the Word of God became flesh and dwelt among men and was handled by men, and lived in this world. And at the age of thirty-three years, He paid the debt on Calvary's cross. Oh beloved, if we expect to reign with Him, we must suffer with Him—not that people must be sick or unhealthy or go with a long face, but we must bear all things and keep the faith of Jesus in our hearts. Our lives now are with the suffering Christ, and *"it doth not yet appear what we shall be: but we know that, when he shall appear, we shall be like him; for we shall see him as he is"* (1 John 3:2). Glory to Jesus.

After Jesus introduced Himself to John on the Isle of Patmos, He gave John these blessed messages to the church. John was permitted to see from the beginning of the church age on down to the white throne judgment, the final winding up of the world. He was permitted to see the overcomers. He was permitted to see the millennial reign with Jesus in triumph over the kingdoms of Satan, to see this old world pass away, to see the new heavens and new earth, and the New Jerusalem coming down from God out of heaven. John saw things past, things present, and things in the future. He had witnessed the glory and power of the apostolic church, and saw the falling away of the church, and God sent him to the church with this blessed message, that she should come back to her first love.

THE VISION OF JESUS IN HIS CHURCH

The most striking passage of Scripture in the first chapter of Revelation is where John was permitted to see Jesus walking among the golden candlesticks, which represent the church. Christ is in His church today to fill men and women, to heal their bodies, save and sanctify their souls, and to put His finger upon every wrong and mean thing in the church. His rebuke is against it, for He hates sin today as much as He ever did when He walked by the Sea of Galilee. Glory to His name. Jesus hates impure doctrine just as much as when He rebuked the Pharisees for their impure doctrine.

John beheld Jesus in His glorified body. What a holy scene it was: the Son of God *"clothed with a garment down to the foot, and girt about the paps with a golden girdle. His head and his hairs were white like wool, as white as snow; and his eyes were as a flame of fire"* (Revelation 1:13–14). Hallelujah. There is nothing but purity and holiness in our Savior.

Glory to Jesus. *"And his feet like unto fine brass, as if they burned in a furnace; and his voice as the sound of many waters"* (verse 15), which represents many people. Bless God.

"And he had in his right hand seven stars" (verse 16). This represents His Holy Ghost ministers. Jesus has them in His hand; that is to say that He gave them the authority to preach the gospel and power over devils. All of our authority and power comes from Jesus. It is so sweet when we know that we have authority from Jesus. Bless His holy name. Oh beloved, when we know Jesus Christ has His minister in His hand, we know that minister is a live preacher. Glory to Jesus. Hallelujah. A live minister represents one that is saved, sanctified, and filled with the Holy Spirit. Then the same life, the same authority, that Jesus promised, we will find in his life.

"And out of his mouth went a sharp twoedged sword: and his countenance was as the sun shineth in his strength" (verse 16), the glory of God shining through the blessed Christ. *"And when I saw him, I fell at his feet as dead. And he laid his right hand upon me, saying unto me, Fear not; I am the first and the last"* (verse 17). Praise God, Jesus is alive and because He lives, everyone that gets Christ is alive in the blessed Holy Spirit. The blood of Jesus Christ does give life, power and fire, joy, peace, happiness, and faith. Hallelujah to His name.

"I am he that liveth, and was dead; and, behold, I am alive for evermore" (verse 18). Bless His holy name. He wanted John to know that He was the same One that hung and bled and died and shed His precious blood on Calvary's cross, went down into the grave, and rose again. This ought to make the whole body of Christ's

people everywhere happy to know that Jesus is alive forevermore. Hallelujah to His name.

Then He said, *"And [I] have the keys of hell and of death."* Bless God. No wonder Brother David said, *"Though I walk through the valley of the shadow of death, I will fear no evil: for thou art with me"* (Psalm 23:4). When we get Jesus Christ in our hearts, we can use the Word and it is a comfort to us to know that we have passed from death to life.

Then Jesus told John particularly, *"Write the things which thou hast seen, and the things which are, and the things which shall be hereafter"* (Revelation 1:19).

THE MESSAGE TO THE CHURCH OF EPHESUS

Then He gave John the messages to the seven churches. *"Unto the angel of the church at Ephesus write; These things saith he that holdeth the seven stars in his right hand, who walketh in the midst of the seven golden candlesticks"* (Revelation 2:1). Hallelujah to His name. Ephesus was a city of Asia, quite a commercial city, a city of wealth, refinement, culture, and great learning. It was where John preached and where Paul had labored. Many people there had been saved and baptized with the Spirit. Paul had witnessed a great scene in Ephesus, where he had preached the gospel of the Son of God and of the doctrine of the baptism with the Holy Spirit, and twelve men, after hearing of this blessed doctrine, received water baptism, and when Paul laid his hands on them, they received the baptism with the Holy Ghost and spoke with tongues and prophesied. (See Acts 19:6.)

So Ephesus was a favored place, but the message was sent to it and to all the churches of Asia. This is a true picture of the Lord Jesus's eyes upon the church ever since its beginning, and will be unto the end. We are living near the close of the Gentile age down in the Laodicean period, when the church has become as formal as the Laodiceans. This message was first to the church of Ephesus.

I KNOW THY WORKS

The Lord Jesus said, *"I know thy works"*—God knows our works, He knows our hearts—*"and thy labour, and thy patience, and how thou canst not bear them which are evil: and thou has tried them which say they are apostles, and are not, and hast found them liars: and hast borne, and hast patience, and for my name's sake hast labored, and hast not fainted"* (Revelation 2:2–3). Bless our God. That is more than many churches today could receive from the Master. Jesus commended them for what they had done. He commended them for their faithfulness. He is not like men. He knows our hearts, our trials, and our conditions. But bless God, He does not make any allowance for sin. He hates sin today as much as He ever did. Yet He does not come to destroy us or condemn us, but to seek and to save us.

"*Nevertheless I have somewhat against thee, because thou hast left thy first love*" (verse 4). The Lord does not want anything to get between us and Him. Oh may every precious child in these times that are getting the Holy Spirit not go into apostasy, but may they be a burning and a shining light for God, just as we were when we first received the baptism with the Holy Spirit. God wants us to keep the same anointing that we received and let nothing separate us from Christ.

REPENTANCE

We find Jesus still preaches the same doctrine of repentance that He preached while on earth. In order to get right with God, He says, "*Remember therefore from whence thou art fallen, and repent, and do the first works; or else I will come unto thee quickly, and will remove thy candlestick out of his place, except thou repent*" (verse 5). Dear beloved, if there is anything wrong in your life and Jesus has His finger upon it, oh may you give it up, for Jesus is truly in His church today. This is the Holy Ghost dispensation and He does convince men of sin, righteousness, and the judgment, and if we will be honest, God will bless us.

TO THE CHURCH TODAY

When a church or mission finds that the power of God begins to leave, they should come as a whole and confess, and let all get down before God and repent and pray to God until the old-time fire and power and love come back again. Many times, the Holy Spirit will leave an assembly, mission, or church because the pastor grieves Him, and sometimes not only the pastor, but the whole body commences backbiting, whispering, tattling, or prejudice and partiality creep in, until the whole becomes corrupted, and Jesus is just ready to spew them out of His mouth. But, oh beloved, let us then come to the second chapter of Revelation and see what Jesus says to the assembly. He expects to find the church, when He comes back to earth again, just as full of fire and power and the signs following, as it was when He organized it on the day of Pentecost. Bless His holy name. May God help all His precious praying children to get back to the old Pentecostal power and fire and love. The church at that time was as terrible as an army with banners. She conquered every power of evil. Hypocrites were not able to remain in it any more than Ananias and Sapphira. (See Acts 5:1–10.) God gave such wonderful love to His people.

Then He gave messengers to every church, showing that Jesus's eyes are upon every church. His finger this day is upon every heart that does not measure to the fullness of holiness. God wants a holy church and all wrong cleansed away—fornication and adultery, two wives, two husbands, not paying grocery bills, water bills, furniture bills, coal bills, gas bills, and all honest bills. God wants His people to be true and holy and He will work. Nothing can hinder. Bless His holy name.

I thank God for this wonderful message to the church, a message from heaven, given by Jesus to show that He is in the church, that He does walk among the golden candlesticks. He is in heaven, but through the power of the Holy Spirit, He walks in the church today. Nothing can be hidden from His pure eyes. He wants people to live the highest and deepest consecration to Him. He does not want their love for him divided. Their first love is to Him.

IMPURE DOCTRINE

We find many of Christ's people tangled up in these days, committing spiritual fornication as well as physical fornication and adultery. They say, "Let us all come together; if we are not one in doctrine, we can be one in spirit." But, dear ones, we cannot all be one, except through the Word of God. He says, *"But this thou hast, that thou hatest the deeds of the Nicolaitanes, which I also hate"* (Revelation 2:6). I suppose that the apostolic church at Ephesus allowed people that were not teaching straight doctrine, not solid in the Word of God, to remain in fellowship with them; and Jesus saw that a little heaven would leaven the whole, and His finger was right upon that impure doctrine. It had to be removed out of the church or He would remove the light and break the church up. When we find things wrong, contrary to Scripture, I care not how dear it is, it must be removed. We cannot bring Agag among the children of Israel, for God says he must die. (See 1 Samuel 15.) Saul saved Agag, which represented saving himself, the carnal nature or old man; but Samuel said Agag must die, and he drew his sword and slew him. Christ's precious Word, which is the sword of Samuel, puts all carnality and sin to death. It means perfect obedience to walk with the Lord. There are many people in these last days that are not going to live a Bible salvation, they are going to take chances. But may God help everyone, if their tight hand or right eye offend them, to cast it from them. It is better to enter into life maimed than for soul and body to be cast into hell fire.

The Lord says, *"He that hath an ear, let him hear what the Spirit saith unto the churches; To him that overcometh will I give to eat of the tree of life, which is in the midst of the paradise of God"* (Revelation 2:7). Oh beloved, if we expect to reign with the Lord and Savior Jesus Christ, we must overcome the world, the flesh, and the devil. There will be many that will be saved but will not be full overcomers to reign on this earth with our Lord. He will give us power to overcome if we are willing. Bless His holy name.

W. J. SEYMOUR
Vol. 1, No. 11

SEVENTEEN

TO THE MARRIED

1 CORINTHIANS 7

In these last days, so many deceptive spirits are in the world, that we have felt impressed by the blessed Holy Spirit to write a letter on the seventh chapter of first Corinthians, that blessed letter which Paul has sent to the church.

The Corinthian church was one of Paul's most gifted churches, and just as it is today, where a church is very gifted, the only safeguard from deceptive spirits is by rightly dividing the Word of God, to keep out fanaticism. We may let down on some lines and rise on others, but God wants everything to be balanced by the Word of God. Paul writing to Timothy says, *"Hold fast the form of sound words, which thou has heard of me, in faith and love which is in Christ Jesus. That good thing which was committed unto thee keep by the Holy Ghost which dwelleth in us"* (2 Timothy 1:13–14). And again he says, *"But continue thou in the things which thou hast learned and hast been assured of, knowing of whom thou hast learned them; and that from a child thou hast known the holy scriptures, which are able to make thee wise unto salvation through faith which is in Christ Jesus. All scripture is given by inspiration of God, and is profitable for doctrine, for reproof, for correction, for instruction in righteousness: that the man of God may be perfect, thoroughly furnished unto all good works"* (2 Timothy 3:14–17). So the Lord God wants us to search and compare Scriptures with Scriptures.

This Corinthian church had run into freeloveism, and a good many -isms. Great division had arisen in it; it had split into several parts, and Paul had to settle them down into the Word of God. He writes this letter to them, for they had got into awful trouble.

Paul tells them in the first verse of this chapter to avoid immorality. He says, *"Now concerning the things whereof ye wrote unto me: It is good for a man not to touch a woman"* (1 Corinthians 7:1). He does not mean a married man here; he means a man that is single, as verses

8 and 26 show. He says, *"Every man hath his proper gift of God"* (verse 7). And to those that can receive this gift, Paul writes, *"I say therefore to the unmarried and widows, it is good for them if they abide even as I"* (verse 8). That is to say, by living a single life, they would have more power in the Spirit. He writes this to the church, to any who are saved, sanctified, and filled with the Holy Spirit. Paul thought it was best, but he showed that everyone had his proper gift of God. So he did not put any bondage upon the people of Christ, because he had no Scripture for it.

He says in the second and third verses, *"Nevertheless, to avoid fornication, let every man have his own wife, and let every woman have her own husband. Let the husband render unto the wife due benevolence: and likewise also the wife unto the husband."* This of course means conjugal intercourse between man and wife. *"The wife hath not power of her own body, but the husband: and likewise also the husband hath not power of his own body, but the wife"* (verse 4). That is to say, that the husband has no authority to live separated, without the consent of his wife; and the wife has no authority of herself to live separated without the husband. Then Paul says in the fifth verse, *"Defraud ye not one the other, except it be with consent for a time, that ye may give yourselves to fasting and prayer; and come together again, that Satan tempt you not for your incontinency."*

That is to say that every wife and husband should abstain from impurity, and give themselves to fasting for a time. It should be by mutual agreement between the two to fast for power and blessing, and many times to avoid impurity. But he advised them to come again, *"that Satan tempt you not for your incontinency."* Paul here does not make this a law, but as one that had the Holy Spirit, he gives them this advice. He adds in the sixth verse, *"But I speak this by permission, and not of commandment."* In Romans 1:26, Paul shows there is a natural use for a wife, which is not lust. Speaking of the ungodly, he says, *"For this cause God gave them up unto vile affections: for even their women did change the natural use into that which is against nature."* May God help us to be clear teachers of His Word.

"I would that all men were even as I myself. But every man hath his proper gift of God, one after this manner, and another after that" (1 Corinthians 7:7). Paul is referring here to Matthew 19:12, where Jesus told the Pharisees that there were some men that were born eunuchs from their mother's womb (that is to say, unable to have wives); some have been made eunuchs of men (for other advantages in life); and there were some eunuchs *"for the kingdom of heaven's sake."* Men had prayed to God for this gift or blessing, just as Paul, who said he wished all men were like him; he no doubt became a eunuch for the kingdom of heaven's sake. Jesus Himself said, *"All men cannot receive this saying, save they to whom it is given"* (Matthew 19:11). So Jesus did not put any bondage on

men and women, but a man today that has received the power to become a eunuch for the kingdom of heaven's sake can live a single life with all holiness and purity. Praise our God!

We must rightly divide the Scriptures and compare Scripture with Scripture so that there be no confusion and no deceptive spirit or wrong teaching may creep in. Paul says, *"But this I say, brethren, the time is short: it remaineth, that both they that have wives be as though they had none; and they that weep, as though they wept not; and they that rejoice, as though they rejoiced not; and they that buy, as though they possessed not; and they that use the world, as not abusing it: for the fashion of this world passeth away"* (1 Corinthians 7:29–31). Bless the Lord! Now Paul, in speaking this, did not put any bondage on mothers to fear that they would not be able to meet Jesus in His coming because they were bringing forth children. Mothers and fathers that are saved and sanctified, to whom the Lord has given this gift of bringing forth children, can live a pure and holy life before God and be of the bride of Christ, just as the bishop that teaches this holy Gospel can be the husband of one wife and raise his children in the fear of God.

Married couples who are mutually agreed, having received from the Lord power over both body, soul and spirit, God does not ask them to desire; but may they live as God has called them. Many times, God gives this power to the husband before to the wife.

Many times, the wife has it; but in order to save the husband, she has to submit to the husband. *"For God is not the author of confusion"* (1 Corinthians 14:33). This brings us back to the third verse of this same chapter. Also in Ephesians 5:22, we read, *"Wives, submit your-selves unto your own husbands, as unto the Lord."* Please read on down to verse 33. God does not make the husband the tyrant or cruel sovereign over the wife, neither does He make the wife to exercise tyranny over the husband, but He makes both one. God knows our hearts and our lives.

Someone may ask what Jesus meant in Matthew 24:19, *"And woe unto them that are with child, and to them that give suck in those days!"* Well, beloved, here Jesus's heart was upon the people that would suffer in the awful tribulation that was coming to Jerusalem forty years after His ascension. He says to them, *"But pray ye that your flight be not in the winter, neither on the sabbath day"* (verse 20). Jesus was the Son of God, but He was a man of prayer. He asked His disciples to pray with Him in the garden of Gethsemane. He knew that in the destruction of Jerusalem, if they prayed to God, the Father would not permit it to come to pass in the winter, neither on the Sabbath day.

He knew if it was on the Sabbath day, the Jews would be keeping the old Mosaic law *"of the new moon, or of the sabbath days: which are a shadow of things to come; but the body is of Christ"* (Colossians 2:16–17). The greatest thing that people need in this day is Christ, and then all the days will come in their order and in their place. Jesus knew if their flight occurred on the Sabbath day, all the gates of Jerusalem would be shut and the Christians could not get out, and the mothers could not escape, so His heart went out for the precious women. The Lord Jesus Christ knows all about our struggles. He knows all about our sufferings and our trials. He is touched with every infirmity and He remembers us. Bless His holy name.

May God help everyone that is getting saved to stay within the lids of God's Word and wait on God, and He will make all things right. Now we can give up anything that we see is really of self-gratification. The Lord wants us to be temperate in all things. Bless His holy name. People that are desiring to get the victory over spirit, soul and body, can have it if they will trust God. I have been asked so much on this question, and I can only give what God has revealed to me through His precious Word. Bless His holy name!

W. J. S.
Vol. 1, No. 12

EIGHTEEN

SANCTIFIED ON THE CROSS

"I pray not that thou shouldest take them out of the world, but that thou shouldest keep them from the evil. They are not of the world, even as I am not of the world. Sanctify them through thy truth: thy word is truth" (John 17:15–17). Jesus is still praying this prayer today for every believer to come and be sanctified. Glory to God!

Sanctification makes us one with the Lord Jesus. (See Hebrews 2:11.) Sanctification makes us holy as Jesus is. Then the prayer of Jesus is answered, and we become one with Him, even as He is one with the Father. Bless His holy name. He says again in 1 Thessalonians 4:3, *"For this is the will of God, even your sanctification."* It is His will for every soul to be saved from all sin, actual and original. We get our actual sins cleansed away through the blood of Jesus Christ at the cross, but our original sin we get cleansed on the cross. It must be a real death to the old man.

"Knowing this, that our old man is crucified with him, that the body of sin might be destroyed, that henceforth we should not serve sin. For he that is dead is freed from sin" (Romans 6:6–7). So it takes the death of the old man in order that Christ might be sanctified in us. It is not sufficient to have the old man stunned or knocked down, for he will rise again.

God is calling His people to true holiness in these days. We thank God for the blessed light that He is giving us. He says in 2 Timothy 2:21, *"If a man therefore purge himself from these, he shall be a vessel unto honour, sanctified, and meet for the master's use."* He means for us to be purged from uncleanness and all kinds of sin. Then we shall be it vessel unto honor, sanctified and meet for the Master's use, and prepared unto every good work. Sanctification makes us holy and destroys the breed of sin, the love of sin and carnality. It makes us pure and whiter than snow. Bless His holy name!

The Lord Jesus says, *"Blessed are the pure in heart"* (Matthew 5:8). Sanctification makes us pure in heart. Any man that is saved and sanctified can feel the fire burning in his heart, when he calls on the name of Jesus. Oh, may God help men and women everywhere to lead a holy life, free from sin, for the Holy Spirit seeks to lead you out of sin into the marvelous light of the Son of God.

The Word says, *"Follow peace with all men, and holiness, without which no man shall see the Lord"* (Hebrews 12:14). So, beloved, when we get Jesus Christ our King of Peace in our hearts, we have the almighty Christ, the everlasting Father, the Prince of Peace. *"Thou wilt keep him in perfect peace, whose mind is stayed on thee: because he trusteth in thee"* (Isaiah 26:3). We shall have wisdom, righteousness, and power. For God is righteous in all His ways and holy in all His acts. This holiness means perfect love in our hearts, perfect love that casts out fear. (See 1 John 4:18.)

Brother Paul says in order to become holy and live a holy life, we should *"abstain from all appearance of evil. And the very God of peace sanctify you wholly; and I pray God your whole spirit and soul and body be preserved blameless unto the coming of our Lord Jesus Christ"* (1 Thessalonians 5:22–23).

"To the end he may stablish your hearts unblameable in holiness before God, even our Father, at the coming of our Lord Jesus Christ with all his saints" (1 Thessalonians 3:13). Bless His holy name. Oh, beloved, after you have received the light, it is holiness or hell. God is calling for men and women in these days that will live a holy life free from sin. We should remain before God until

His all cleansing blood makes us holy, body, soul, and spirit.

W. J. S.
Vol. 1, No. 12

NINETEEN

THE BAPTISM WITH THE HOLY GHOST

The Azusa standard of the baptism with the Holy Ghost is according to the Bible in Acts 1:5, Acts 1:8, Acts 2:4, and Luke 24:49. Bless His holy name. Hallelujah to the Lamb for the baptism with the Holy Ghost and fire and speaking in tongues as the Spirit gives utterance. Jesus gave the church at Pentecost a great lesson of how to carry on a revival, and it would be well for every church to follow Jesus's standard of the baptism with the Holy Ghost and fire.

"And when the day of Pentecost was fully come, they were all with one accord in one place" (Acts 2:1). Oh, beloved, there is where the secret is: one accord, one place, one

heart, one soul, one mind, one prayer. If God can get a people anywhere in one accord and in one place, of one heart, mind, and soul, believing for this great power, it will fall and Pentecostal results will follow. Glory to God!

Apostolic Faith doctrine means one accord, one soul, one heart. May God help every child of His to live in Jesus's prayer, *"That they all may be one; as thou, Father, art in me, and I in thee, that they also may be one in us: that the world may believe that thou hast sent me"* (John 17:21). Praise God! Oh, how my heart cries out to God in these days that He would make every child of His see the necessity of living in John 17, that we may be one in the body of Christ, as Jesus has prayed.

When we are sanctified through the truth, then we are one in Christ, and we can get into one accord for the gift or power of the Holy Ghost, and God will come in like a rushing mighty wind and fill every heart with the power of the Holy Spirit. Glory to His holy name. Bless God! Oh, how I praise Him for this wonderful salvation that is spreading over this great earth. The baptism of the Holy Ghost brings the glory of God to our hearts.

THE HOLY GHOST IS POWER

There is a great difference between a sanctified person and one that is baptized with the Holy Ghost and fire. A sanctified person is cleansed and filled with divine love, but the one that is baptized with the Holy Ghost has the power of God on his soul and has power with God and men, power over all the kingdoms of Satan and over all his emissaries.

God can take a worm and thresh a mountain. Glory to God. Hallelujah!

In all Jesus's great revivals and miracles, the work was wrought by the power of the Holy Ghost flowing through His sanctified humanity. When the Holy Ghost comes and takes us as His instruments, this is the power that convicts men and women and causes them to see that there is a reality in serving Jesus Christ. Oh, beloved, we ought to thank God that He has made us the tabernacles of the Holy Ghost. When you have the Holy Ghost, you have an empire, a power within yourself. Elijah was a power in himself through the Holy Ghost. He brought down fire from heaven. (See 1 Kings 18:37–38.) So when we get the power of the Holy Ghost, we will see the heavens open and the Holy Ghost power falling on earth, power over sickness, diseases, and death.

The Lord never revoked the commission He gave to His disciples, *"Heal the sick, cleanse the lepers, raise the dead"* (Matthew 10:8), and He is going to perform these things if He can get a people in unity. The Holy Spirit is power with God and man. You have power with God as Elijah had. God put man over all His works, but we know that when Adam sinned, he lost a great deal of his power. But now through the blood of Jesus, He says, *"Behold, I give unto you power to tread on serpents and scorpions, and over all the powers of the enemy"* (Luke 10:19). The Lord Jesus wants a church, when He comes back to earth, just like the one He started when He left the earth and organized it on the day of Pentecost.

TARRY IN ONE ACCORD

Oh, may every child of God seek his real personal Pentecost, stop quibbling, and come to the standard that Jesus laid down for us in Acts 2:2, *"And suddenly there came a sound from heaven as of a rushing mighty wind, and it filled all the house where they were sitting."* Glory to God! Oh, beloved, if you wait on God for this baptism of the Holy Ghost just now, and can get two or three people together that are sanctified through the blood of Christ, and all get into one accord, God will send the baptism of the Holy Ghost upon your souls as the rain falls from heaven. You may not have a preacher to come to you and preach the doctrine of the Holy Ghost and fire, but you can obey Jesus's saying in the passage. *"Where two or three are gathered together in my name, there am I in the midst of them"* (Matthew 18:20). This is Jesus's baptism; and if two or three are gathered together in His name and pray for the baptism of the Holy Ghost, they can have it this day or this night because it is the promise of the Father. Glory to God!

This was the Spirit that filled the house as a rushing mighty wind. The Holy Ghost is typified by wind, air, breath, life, or fire. *"And there appeared unto them cloven tongues like as of fire, and it sat upon each of them. And they were all filled with the Holy Ghost, and began to speak with other tongues, as the Spirit gave them utterance"* (Acts 2:3–4). So, beloved, when you get your personal Pentecost, the signs will follow in speaking with tongues as the Spirit gives utterance. This is true. Wait on God and you will find it a truth in your own life. God's promises are true and sure.

THE BAPTISM FALLS ON A CLEAN HEART

Jesus is our example. *"And Jesus being full of the Holy Ghost returned from Jordan, and was led by the Spirit"* (Luke 4:1). We find in reading the Bible that the baptism with the Holy Ghost and fire falls on a clean, sanctified life, for we see according to the Scriptures that Jesus was *"holy, harmless, undefiled"* (Hebrews 7:26), and filled with wisdom and favor with God and man, before God anointed Him with the Holy Ghost and power. For in Luke 2:40 we read, *"The child [Jesus] grew, and waxed strong in spirit, filled with wisdom: and the grace of God was upon him,"* and in Luke 2:52, *"And Jesus increased in wisdom and stature, and in favour with God and man."*

After Jesus was empowered with the Holy Ghost at the Jordan, He returned in the power of the Spirit into Galilee, and there went out a fame of Him through all the region round about. Glory to God! He was not any more holy or any more meek, but had greater authority. *"And he taught in their synagogues, being glorified of all"* (Luke 4:15).

Beloved, if Jesus who was God Himself needed the Holy Ghost to empower Him for His ministry and His miracles, how much more do we children need the Holy Ghost baptism today. Oh, that men and women would tarry for the baptism with the Holy Ghost and fire upon their souls, that the glory may be seen upon them just as it was upon the disciples on the day of Pentecost in the fiery emblem of tongues.

The tongues of fire represented the great Shekinah glory. So today the Shekinah glory rests day and night upon those who are baptized with the Holy Ghost, while He abides in their souls. For His presence is with us. Glory to His name. I thank Him for this wonderful salvation. Let us ring His praises through all the world that all men may know that the Comforter has come. Bless His dear name!

JESUS'S FIRST SERMON AFTER HIS BAPTISM

"And he came to Nazareth, where he had been brought up: and, as his custom was, he went into the synagogue on the sabbath day, and stood up for to read. And there was delivered unto him the book of the prophet Esaias [Isaiah]. And when he had opened the book, he found the place where

it is written, The Spirit of the Lord is upon me, because he hath anointed me to preach the gospel to the poor; he hath sent me to heal the brokenhearted, to preach deliverance to the captives, and recovering of sight to the blind, to set at liberty them that are bruised, to preach the acceptable year of the Lord" (Luke 4:16–19). Hallelujah. Glory to God! This is Jesus's sermon after His baptism with the Holy Ghost, preaching in the synagogue. He acknowledged that the Spirit of God was upon Him.

Jesus was the Son of God and born of the Holy Ghost and filled with the Holy Ghost from His mother's womb, but the baptism with the Holy Ghost came upon His sanctified humanity at the Jordan. In His humanity, He needed the Third Person of the Trinity to do His work. And He could truly say that His fingers became instruments of the Holy Ghost to cast out devils.

THE HOLY SPIRIT FLOWS THROUGH PURE CHANNELS

If men and women today will consecrate themselves to God, and get their hands and feet, eyes and affections, body and soul, all sanctified, how the Holy Ghost will use such people. He will find pure channels to flow through sanctified avenues for His power. People will be saved, sanctified, healed, and baptized with the Holy Ghost and fire.

The baptism with the Holy Ghost comes through our Lord and Savior Jesus Christ by faith in His Word.

In order to receive it, we must first be sanctified. Then we can become His witnesses unto the uttermost parts of the earth. You will never have an experience to measure with Acts 2:4 and Acts 2:16–17 until you get your personal Pentecost or the baptism with the Holy Ghost and fire. (See Matthew 3:11.)

This is the latter rain that God is pouring out upon His humble children in the last days. We are preaching a gospel that measures with the Great Commission that Jesus gave His disciples on the day when He arose from the dead: "*Go ye therefore, and teach all nations, baptizing them in the name of the Father, and of the Son, and of the Holy Ghost: teaching them to observe all things whatsoever I have commanded you: and, lo, I am with you always, even unto the end of the world. Amen*" (Matthew 28:19–20). They received the power to measure with this commission on the day of Pentecost. (See Acts 2:4.) Bless the Lord. Oh, how I bless God to see His mighty power manifested in these last days. God wants His people to receive the baptism with the Holy Ghost and fire.

W. J. S.
Vol. 2, No. 13

TWENTY

THE HOLY GHOST AND THE BRIDE

We read in Revelation 22:17, "*The Spirit and the bride say, Come.*" Oh, how sweet it is for us to have this blessed privilege of being a coworker with the Holy Ghost. He inspires us with faith in God's Word and endues us with power for service for the Master. Bless His dear name!

Every man and woman that receives the baptism with the Holy Ghost is the bride of Christ. They have a missionary spirit for saving souls. They have the spirit of Pentecost. Glory to God!

"And let him that heareth say, Come. And let him that is athirst come. And whosoever will, let him take the water of life freely" (Revelation 22:17). Oh, what a blessed text. The bride of Christ is calling the thirsty to come to Jesus because this is the work of the Holy Ghost in the believer. He intercedes for the lost; He groans for them.

The Spirit also calls the believer to come to Jesus and get sanctified. He points the sanctified to Jesus for his baptism with the Holy Ghost. When you are baptized with the Holy Ghost, you will have power to call sinners to Jesus, and they will be saved, and sanctified, and baptized with the Holy Ghost and fire. Amen!

Christ's bride is pure and spotless. *"Thou art all fair, my love; there is no spot in thee"* (Song of Solomon 4:7). Christ's bride is clean, free from sin and all impurity. He gave Himself for her, that He might sanctify and cleanse the church with the washing of water by the Word, that He might present it to Himself a glorious church, not having spot or wrinkle or any such thing, but that it should be holy and without blemish. (See Ephesians 5:25–27.) Christ's bride has but one husband. (See 2 Corinthians 11:2.) She is subject to Him. (See Ephesians 5:25.) The Bridegroom is the Son of God. (See 2 Corinthians 11:2.)

We are married to Christ now in the Spirit. (See Romans 7:2–4.) Not only when He comes are we married to Christ, but also right now, if you are sanctified and baptized with the Holy Ghost and fire, you are married to Him already. God has a people to measure up to the Bible standard in this great salvation. Bless His holy name. Amen!

W. J. S.
Vol. 2, No. 13

ABOUT ROBERTS LIARDON

Roberts Liardon was born in Tulsa, Oklahoma, while his mother was a charter class student at Oral Roberts University. For the distinction of being the first male child born to an ORU student, his parents named him Roberts in honor of its founder, Oral Roberts.

Dr. Liardon was called into the ministry at a very young age. Kathryn Kuhlman prophesied to him as a young boy that he was called by God to serve in ministry to the church. Subsequently, he preached his first public sermon at the age of thirteen and began lecturing in Christian colleges and universities about his research on *God's Generals* at age fifteen.

At sixteen, Dr. Liardon began his media ministry by launching a radio program in Tulsa, and at seventeen he wrote his first book, *I Saw Heaven*, which initially sold 1.5 million copies. This book was Dr. Liardon's account of his visit to heaven as an eight-year-old boy, and it catapulted him into the public eye.

Shortly after the publication of *I Saw Heaven*, God inspired Dr. Liardon to write a best-selling book series, based on his *God's Generals* research. This series chronicles the lives and ministries of some of the church's greatest leaders in revival movements throughout the world and through the centuries. One of the unique aspects of the series is that it tells why they succeeded as well as why some failed. Later, Dr. Liardon produced several video series based on these books. This established him as a leading Protestant church historian, a reputation he continues to merit.

The *God's Generals* series brought him international attention. Twice, he was awarded the prestigious title of "Outstanding Young Man of America." He met with President Ronald Reagan, British Prime Minister Margaret Thatcher, and Dr. Billy Graham. He has received letters of commendation from many others he has not met personally, including a letter from then President George and Laura Bush, honoring him for his commitment and contribution to improve the quality of life in his community.

In his mid-twenties, Dr. Liardon built one of the fastest growing churches in the U.S. and established his first accredited Bible college. From this ministry, he founded over forty churches, built five international Bible colleges, and assisted the poor and needy in his community, throughout America, and around the globe. He sent close to 500 humanitarian teams of men and women to various nations. These humanitarian teams not only shared the good news of Jesus Christ but also provided food, clothing, and medical assistance. In Namibia, Africa, Dr. Liardon assisted a ministry in starting the first AIDS prevention campaign in public schools there.

As he neared age thirty, Dr. Liardon began a television program, *The High Life*, which was seen worldwide on the Trinity Broadcasting Network. Later, he launched a TV show called *God's Generals with Roberts Liardon*, which aired in over 200 nations on various Christian networks.

As a recognized church historian specializing in revival and reformation movements, Dr. Liardon has one of the world's largest collections of church history memorabilia. It contains rare books, films, photos, voice recordings, and personal effects of church leaders he has researched.

Through the years, he has received spiritual oversight and personal mentorship from great men of God like Dr. Oral Roberts, Dr. Lester Sumrall, Rev. Billy Joe Daugherty, Dr. R. T. Kendall, and Colin Dye. For many years, he has also provided spiritual oversight and accountability to others.

Dr. Liardon's present ministry, Embassy International Church in Orlando, Florida, is an apostolic center to train the next generation and build the church at large. With it, he launched Embassy Global Network, where leaders and believers can come to be blessed and form ministry support networks. He has also established Embassy International churches in Orange County, California, and San Francisco, California.

Dr. Liardon continues to be an internationally best-selling author, having sold over 16 million books, and his works have been translated into over sixty languages. In great demand as a speaker and as a mentor to pastors and leaders, he has ministered in over 127 nations to date. He loves to pray, teach the Word of God, and prophesy to bless God's people.

As an author, public speaker, spiritual leader, church historian, and humanitarian, Dr. Roberts Liardon speaks to a current generation of believers who want to draw closer to the heart and mind of God and impact their communities and the nations of the world through the gospel of Jesus Christ.

You may contact Dr. Liardon at:

www.robertsliardon.com

Facebook: Roberts Liardon Official

Twitter: Roberts Liardon

Instagram: robertsliardon_official

U.S. Office:

Roberts Liardon Ministries
P.O. Box 781888
Orlando, FL 32878
Email: admin@robertsliardon.org

UK and Europe Office:

Roberts Liardon Ministries
UK, 22 Notting Hill Gate, Suite 125
London W11 3JE, UK
Email: admin@robertsliardon.org

Welcome to Our House!

We Have a Special Gift for You ...

It is our privilege and pleasure to share in your love of Christian classics by publishing books that enrich your life and encourage your faith.

To show our appreciation, we invite you to sign up to receive a specially selected **Reader Appreciation Gift**, with our compliments. Just go to the Web address at the bottom of this page.

God bless you as you seek a deeper walk with Him!

WE HAVE A GIFT FOR YOU

whpub.me/classicthx

WHITAKER
HOUSE